Tom
Ruffles

GW00367336

Brief Lives.
Oscar Wilde

Amy T. Ryder '08

Brief Lives:
Oscar Wilde

Richard Canning

ET REMOTISSIMA PROPE

Brief Lives
Published by Hesperus Press Limited
4 Rickett Street, London SW6 1RU
www.hesperuspress.com

First published by Hesperus Press Limited, 2008

Copyright © Richard Canning, 2008
The right of Richard Canning to be identified as the Author of the Work
has been asserted by him in accordance with the Copyright, Designs and
Patents Act 1988.

Designed and typeset by Fraser Muggeridge studio
Printed in Jordan by Jordan National Press

ISBN: 1-84391-905-2
ISBN13: 978-1-84391-905-6

All rights reserved. This book is sold subject to the condition that it shall not
be resold, lent, hired out or otherwise circulated without the express prior
consent of the publisher.

Contents

Childhood: Ireland
1854–74

Oscar Wilde was born in Dublin on 16th October 1854. His parents were socially prominent Anglo-Irish Protestants, each with eclectic interests, a belief in nationalist politics and publishing careers of their own. William Robert Wills Wilde (1815–76), Oscar's father, was a renowned physician specialising in the eye and ear. He had acted as assistant medical commissioner for the Irish Census of 1851, for which he was knighted in 1864. From 1853 he had been Queen Victoria's 'Surgeon Oculist'. He was keen on Celtic legend, publishing several books on it, as well as on Irish topography. He met Jane Francesca Agnes Elgee (1821–96), his wife and Oscar's mother, after she favourably reviewed a book of his in 1849. William knew much more about his homeland than most, gathering superstitions and folktales from poorer patients in lieu of fees. These were later collected by his wife and published. He led a visit by the British Association to the Aran Islands in 1857, and the Governor of Uppsala was so impressed he invited the Wildes to Sweden. William was granted the Order of the Polar Star, a medal he wore ostentatiously in Dublin.

Jane Elgee became politicised by the Great Famine of 1845–9. This had brought many converts, including the Anglo-Irish, to the nationalist cause. Elgee adopted the Italian word *Speranza* – 'hope' – as her *nom de plume*, and frequently wrote patriotic verse for *The Nation*, mouthpiece of the Young Ireland movement. William's nationalism was reflected in less direct ways – through his travel writings, for example. He also argued in a book dedicated to Swift that Ireland's most revered writer had been ill, not insane, in his last years.

They married on 12th November 1851. A first son, William Robert Kingsbury Wills Wilde – 'Willie' – was born in September 1852. Oscar Fingal O'Flahertie Wills Wilde was born two years later at the then modest family home, 21 Westland Row. Wilde's first two names were inspired by Irish legend. Jane wrote to a friend that she found the name 'Oscar Fingal Wilde' 'grand, misty, and Ossianic', a reference to Ossian, son of Finn in Irish mythology. 'O'Flahertie' came from a noble Galway name, pointing to her husband's partial west coast ancestry. Both sons took the name 'Wills', which referred to their father's favourite playwright.

When her second son was eight months old, Jane presciently described him as 'a great stout creature who minds nothing but growing fat'. Several friends later wrote that Jane had wanted a girl. She is said to have dressed and treated Oscar as a daughter for the first decade, though this was then common. Otherwise little is known of his first years. The family remained prosperous. His father taught Oscar to fish. At one point, fighting with Willie and another boy, he broke his arm. There was German and French help in the house, and Oscar and Willie became fluent in both languages. In the summer, the Wildes vacationed in the south, generally in County Waterford. On one holiday, the young Oscar befriended another boy, Edward Carson, on the beach. It was Carson who later became Wilde's legal nemesis.

Jane finally gave birth to a daughter two years later. Isola Francesca Emily Wilde was born in April 1857 at the family's new, more prestigious address. 1 Merrion Square North was a large Georgian townhouse, also serving as William's medical practice. The practice was shared by William's oldest, illegitimate son, Henry Wilson, discreetly referred to as a 'cousin' of his boys. In fact, William fathered two other children prior to his marriage, Emily and Mary, both of whom died in 1871 in a fire.

William earned his living not only from the practice, but also, from 1844, by founding and running the pioneering St Mark's Hospital for Diseases of the Eye and Ear. He wrote standard reference works like *Aural Surgery* (1853) and *Epidemic Ophthalmia* (1851). Still, his professional pre-eminence provoked antagonism. W.B. Yeats recounted a story that William had extracted a man's eyes, set them on a plate meaning to reinsert them, only to watch them being eaten by a cat.

Oscar's father was a slight, unkempt figure with an ugly beard, whose personal hygiene was sometimes criticised. Jane, however, was especially elegant and statuesque. Almost six feet tall, she towered over her husband. She longed, she said, 'to make a sensation'. Indeed, she celebrated extremity in general. 'I should like', Jane once wrote, 'to rage through life – this orthodox creeping is too tame for me.' Her extravagance in dress and manner was matched by a capacity for self-reinvention. Of ordinary, lower middle-class origins, she nonetheless claimed that her family name Elgee was a corruption of the Italian 'Algiati', a variant of 'Alighieri'. Thus, she implied, her direct ancestor was Italy's most celebrated poet, Dante Alighieri. A statue of the Reverend Charles Maturin, author of the gothic novel *Melmoth the Wanderer* and a distant uncle of Jane's, stood prominently in the hallway. Later, released from prison, the disgraced Oscar would adopt Maturin's character's surname, signing himself 'Sebastian Melmoth'.

Just as his mother was prone to ironic exaggeration, Oscar gained a reputation for embroidering the truth at school. A fellow pupil recalled, '[r]omantic imagination was strong in him, but there was always something in his telling of such a tale to suggest that he felt his hearers were not really being taken in.' Jane at times signed off as 'Speranza', at others, as 'Francesca Speranza'. Either was preferable to her plain first name. She invariably claimed her birth year as 1826, a date still commonly cited today. No records exist to contradict this, but an application for funding made late in life reveals that Jane invariably shaved five years off her natural age. Her son would soon be imitating her example.

Jane took advantage of Merrion Square's opulence, regularly holding afternoon receptions for a hundred guests or more. Academics, politicians, writers and performers were always around during Oscar's childhood. Even Wilde's legal travails would replicate his mother's own thirst for drama. The editor of *The Nation* allowed her to pen a number of editorials, one of which was cited in a legal dispute which otherwise did not involve Jane. When her words were wrongly attributed to another writer, however, Jane stood up in the gallery and exclaimed: 'I, and I alone, am the culprit, if culprit there be.' She was reprimanded by the judge but her point ran home. His mother would later argue strongly that Oscar stay and defend himself with honour in the trials.

Romantically speaking, Jane was a free-thinker. She forgave her husband's past readily, and, as an old woman, once told a youth, 'When you are as old as I, young man, you will know there is only one thing in the world worth living for, and that is sin.' She scorned bourgeois values. Asked if she would speak to someone called 'respectable', she replied, 'It is only tradespeople who are respectable. We are above respectability.' In 1863, with similar hauteur, Jane abruptly ceased talking to Mary Travers, who had helped in the household since Oscar's birth. Travers had also been a patient of William's, and reacted to the spurning by alleging that he had chloroformed and raped her during surgery in 1862, as well as previously taking advantage of her when Jane was pregnant.

Mary wrote a pamphlet full of these allegations, which prompted Jane to write to Mary's father, accusing her of lies and extortion. Mary launched a £2000 writ against 'Lady Wilde' – as she now was – for libel and missing income. Although, in December 1864, Mary won in the courts, it was a Pyrrhic victory. She was given a farthing in damages, and was socially disgraced. William had to find £2000 in legal costs, true, but the practice boomed after the publicity. Jane wrote to everyone, insisting on Mary Travers' madness. The scandal provoked ribald comment.

By now Oscar and Willie were boarders at Portora Royal School, Enniskillen, far in the Protestant north. The historic school had strong links with Trinity College, Dublin, and was a preferred destination for the offspring of well-to-do Anglo-Irish Protestants. Oscar's mother was keen on its reputation as the 'Eton of Ireland'. When he was sent, just short of ten, Oscar was younger than most of his peers. He was, at first, in the shadow of his brother – as he must have been at home, where Jane would refer to Willie as 'my kingdom'. By the time Willie was set to leave Portora, however, he had been eclipsed academically by Oscar. They were ranked in Classics as thirteenth and fourth respectively. The subject would always be Oscar's best.

Oscar gave nicknames to the other boys, a habit he never gave up. His skill at reading was swiftly noted. In 1889, he recalled his school years:

I was looked upon as a prodigy by my associates because quite frequently, I would, for a wager, read a three-volume novel in half an hour so closely as to be able to give an accurate résumé of the plot of the story; by one hour's reading I was enabled to give a fair narrative of the incidental scenes and the most pertinent dialogue.

His gift for memorising other people's words, and for reproducing them verbatim, would later be honed into dinner talk and even a sort of literary plagiarism. Once, Robbie Ross accused him of being a 'literary thief', to which Oscar grandly replied, 'My dear Robbie, when I see a monstrous tulip with *four* petals in someone else's garden, I am impelled to grow a monstrous tulip with *five* wonderful petals, but that is no reason why someone should grow a tulip with only *three* petals.' At school, as well as devouring the Classics and literary fiction, Wilde read historical romances for pleasure, including Meinhold's *Sidonia the*

Sorceress, translated into English by his mother. He instructed himself in the artistic questions of the day, demanding of one master, 'What is a realist?' As an author, he later set himself against everything 'realism' stood for.

Wilde's schooling seems otherwise to have been unexceptional. He relished his parents buying him large-paper editions of the school textbooks, which, beautifully bound, were quite unlike the other boys'. Only one handwritten letter survives from his time at Portora – from a thirteen-year-old Oscar, addressed to his mother, hinting at the author's incipient dandyism, 'The flannel shirts you sent in the hamper are both Willie's, mine are one quite scarlet and the other lilac, but it is too early to wear them yet, the weather is too hot.' A classmate later recalled that Wilde was 'more careful in his dress than any other boy'. In the letter, Oscar also asked after a new volume of his mother's sprightly national-ist verse, in which she had written a dedication to her boys:

I made them indeed
Speak plain the word country. I taught them, no doubt,
That country's a thing one should die for at need.

Oscar would be attracted to martyrdom and sacrifice, though not in defence of one's country. He would also cherish giving and receiving dedications, though a good number of these would later cause misunderstandings.

Oscar was an achiever at Portora, but not ostentatiously so. In 1866, he was prizeman in the Junior School. In 1869, he came third in Scripture. He would distinguish himself in his final years with sudden, breathtaking summaries and translations of the ancient texts studied. He won a prize for his understanding of Aeschylus' *Agamemnon*, a work Oscar often cited. 1870 saw the Carpenter Prize for Greek Testament. In 1871, Wilde won a scholarship to study Classics at Trinity College, Dublin. His name appeared in gold on the school notice board. (In 1895, it was painted out.)

On 23rd February 1867, tragedy struck the family. Oscar's nine-year-old sister Isola had become gravely ill with fever. Recovery seemed likely at first, and she had been sent to re-cuperate with her uncle in rural Edgeworthstown. When Isola's health deteriorated again, word was sent, but her parents arrived only to see her pass away. Oscar – described by Isola's doctor as 'an affectionate, gentle, retiring, dreamy boy' – was hit hard. He would visit her grave often, and wrote a poem much later, *'Requiescat'*, recording his suffering at the loss of 'She that was young and fair / Fallen to dust'.

Willie was in his final year at Trinity College when Oscar arrived there in 1873. The elder brother had won a medal for Ethics, and went on to study Law in London unsuccessfully before returning to the Bar in Ireland. Edward Carson was also at Trinity, alongside a large set from Portora. Oscar was tutored and befriended by Rev. John Pentland Mahaffy, Professor of Ancient History. Mahaffy inspired his pupil to be proficient in Greek after three years – he was soon among the leading students, and sometimes named as the best in the year. In 1873, Wilde won one of ten Foundation Scholarships. His outgoing achievement was winning the prestigious Berkeley Gold Medal in Greek.

Mahaffy was a robust extrovert – tall like Oscar, thirty-two, rejoicing in the nickname of 'the General'. He knew several European monarchs, and doubtless encouraged Oscar in learn-ing, wit and social confidence. He would later suffer the ignominy of seeing his study in the art of fine conversation unfavourably reviewed by his former pupil. Oscar lamented that Mahaffy could not write as well as he could talk. They were tem-peramental opposites even in college, yet Wilde was cognisant of Mahaffy's benign influence, recalling him in 1893 as 'my first and best teacher'. Oscar also helped Mahaffy with the editing – and, occasionally, writing – of his study *Social Life in Greece from Homer to Menander* (1874). The book bravely touched on male homosexuality, though Mahaffy stressed the generally Platonic attachments between men in Greek culture. A phrase in the book contesting contemporary opinions regarding same-sex relations has often been read as distinctly Wildean, and possibly written by Oscar himself, 'As to the epithet *unnatural*, the Greeks would answer probably, that all civilization was unnatural.' A second edition of Mahaffy's volume omitted the more scandalous references to 'Greek love', as it was informally known. (Oxford's Walter Pater, the next comparable influence on Wilde, was similarly compelled in 1877 to suppress the 'Conclusion' to his 1873 book *The Renaissance*.)

Oscar was also drawn to contemporary literature and culture. Swinburne, an early English exponent of the cryptic, mystical French Symbolist movement, became his favourite poet. Wilde paid tribute to him later in his own poem 'The Garden of Eros'. He would get to know Swinburne personally; Oscar's copy of *Studies in Song* (1880) contains a written dedication. He revered the paintings, writings and example of the Pre-Raphaelite Brotherhood, those of Edward Burne-Jones and Dante Gabriel Rossetti especially, and followed Oxford art historian John Ruskin's advocacy of them. Their ideas were circulated in Trinity's Philosophical Society, which Oscar joined. He also read John Addington Symonds' *Studies of the Greek Poets*, the first volume of which appeared in 1873. Oscar reviewed the second, of 1876, acclaiming 'all the picturesqueness and loveliness of words that we admire so much in Mr Ruskin and Mr Pater'. Mahaffy, meanwhile, mistrusted Symonds' motives. Symonds would go on, discreetly, to lobby for the legitimacy of 'Greek love'. He had written a bold pamphlet on it, *A Problem in Greek Ethics*, even if he did not dare circulate it. Symonds provided a critical bridge for Wilde between contemporaneous aesthetic values and ancient cultures. The Greeks, he argued, had lacked ethical laws because they governed themselves instead by 'aesthesis' – their sense of what was seemly and beautiful.

At this time, Oscar was increasingly drawn both to the ritual and argument of Roman Catholicism. Though Protestant, his mother had, oddly, had both sons baptised in a Catholic church when Oscar was about eight. But there was clearly no tolerance for spiritual waywardness from his father. It may only have been William's threats to disinherit him that prevented Oscar from converting. Mahaffy, himself Protestant, suggested to William that his intellectually gifted son might best continue his studies at Anglican Oxford, rather than in Dublin, with its majority Catholic population and the prominent example of the Catholic University. Now University College, Dublin, the institution had as rector between 1854 and 1858 the celebrated Oxford convert John Henry Newman, whose example and writings would mean much to Wilde.

Oscar was not only subject to Mahaffy's influence at Trinity, however. Its other Classics Professor, Robert Yelverton Tyrrell, was perhaps as formative. Tyrrell encouraged Oscar to contribute to his literary magazine, *Kottabos*, while he was at Trinity and later when he was at Oxford. He conspicuously stood by Wilde following the trials, signing a petition in 1896 for his early release from prison. Mahaffy, however, distanced himself from his former pupil, and did not sign.

In 1874, Oscar sailed to England to take the examination for a Classics 'Demyship' – a scholarship – at Magdalen College, Oxford. It was not only prestigious, but worth £95 per annum for five years. Candidates were to be under twenty on application. Oscar was two months short of his twentieth birthday. Uncertain how to interpret this sanction, and anyhow characteristically insouciant, he gave his age as eighteen. Awaiting the results, Oscar, Willie and Jane went on to London, visiting literary luminaries such as Thomas Carlyle. Oscar was dazzled by his first taste of the metropolis, described by Jane in a letter as 'capital of the world'. The three ventured on to Geneva and Paris, boosted by news of Oscar's triumph. He had easily come top.

That summer in Dublin, Wilde witnessed a sharp decline in his father's health and spirits. Still, his own ambition dominated his thoughts. He was, in any case, Speranza's son. 'You're not quite clever enough for us here, Oscar. Better run up to Oxford,' joked Mahaffy. Wilde duly matriculated on 17th October 1874, one day after turning twenty. As for the lie regarding his age, he and his mother later claimed that he had won the Newdigate Prize for poetry at twenty-two, when he was almost twenty-four. Oscar's marriage certificate repeated the deliberate error. In court, this deceit would give an early advantage to his opponents.

Youth: Oxford, Greece and Italy
1874–8

Oscar – nicknamed 'Hosky' – made the most of Oxford. His undergraduate years were pastoral; Wilde would later recall the 'most flower-like time' of his life. He was conspicuous in his many achievements at Magdalen. Equally, both college and university offered distractions superior to the coarse, relentless drinking at Trinity. Yeats argued that Wilde adopted the mask of the Englishman during his Oxford years, the more strongly to critique the culture he 'joined'. In fact, Wilde's 'Oxford manner', if anything, suggested effortless superiority, being at ease with one's achievements. 'My Irish accent was one of the many things I lost at Oxford,' he later said. (Yet if there was a change, it was probably not so dramatic. The most 'dreadful' version of Dublin English – his mother's term – was presumably never heard in the Merrion Square household anyway.) If Oscar was loyal to Oxford, he thought it was with good reason. The city was charming – 'the most beautiful thing in England'.

Magdalen is among the finest Oxford colleges. The rooms allocated to Wilde did his aesthetic priorities proud, as those at Trinity had not. They were increasingly elaborate, from those in Chaplain's Quad in his first year, in Cloisters in years two and three, and in Kitchen Stairs in his last. He customarily filled them with lilies, symbols of Pre-Raphaelitism. Oscar spent prodigiously to make the furnishings and décor apropos. He famously informed fellow undergraduates, 'I find it harder and

harder every day to live up to my blue china.' These were probably Sèvres vases, accommodating the flowers.

Fitting in was another matter. Wilde was not from the most
celebrated of the English public schools. Most students were now
younger than he, clannish and very confident. An acquaintance
of his, J.E.C. Bodley, later wrote a jaundiced account of Oscar's
early solecisms, though his overall verdict seems apt, that Wilde
was 'a good-natured though unsophisticated young Irishman' in
his first months. As a new arrival, Oscar breached etiquette,
gauchely presenting his card to a third-year athlete. Compared to
later transgressions, this was insignificant. Wilde would learn at
Oxford to make a virtue of misdemeanour. At the same time, he
cherished college formalities – in dress, ceremony and the like –
once he had grasped them.

Wilde was never a fan of sport, but duly watched others play
cricket and run. 'His left leg is a Greek poem', he pronounced of
one athlete. He did train in rowing, but his languor as stroke was
unhelpful. When told to straighten his back, he retorted, 'I am
sure the Greeks never did so at Salamis.' Later, Oscar perfected
the pose of idleness, since: 'the only possible exercise is to talk,
not to walk'. He once admitted to playing no outdoor games
'except dominoes'. At Oxford he did allow himself to partake
in one unusual sport – to be rolled down hills – for which his
increasing corpulence even became an asset. Still, the 'hearties'
at college would always suspect his flamboyance. A common,
though apocryphal, story states that four undergraduates
pounced on Wilde in his rooms, to beat him up and smash his
belongings, as the rest of Magdalen gathered on the stairwell.
They were to be surprised. Wilde is said to have kicked out the
first interloper, punched the second so he doubled over, hurled
the third through the air, and carried the last man to his rooms,
burying him beneath his own furniture.

The university reified individualist learning. This fitted Oscar's
temperamental iconoclasm, independent-mindedness and dis-
trust of ideology. From his 'Commonplace Book', we know that

he continued to read broadly. Wilde consumed works of science and philosophy, referring often to Kant, Hegel, Locke and Mill. Of Oxford dons, he found diverting the writings of the philologist Friedrich Max-Müller, who was translating the *Vedas*, and argued for divine inspiration in human language and thought. Oscar secured a breakfast meeting with him at All Souls. He read English Romantic poets such as Keats and Blake, as well as Dante, Baudelaire and contemporary verse. He identified a worthwhile 'effeminacy and languor and voluptuousness' in Keats and Swinburne which he found properly poetic.

Wilde's influences at Oxford were many, but two were pre-eminent. John Ruskin, Slade Professor of Fine Art, had zealously promoted the virtues of the Pre-Raphaelites, of artisanship and craft, and of medieval industry and achievement. Ruskin informed Wilde's artistic tastes strongly, and became a close friend. Yet it was Brasenose's Walter Pater, at thirty-five a scholar of the next generation, whose words would penetrate more deeply upon Oscar's incipient aestheticism. Wilde would not meet the socially reticent Pater for another two years, but read his *Studies in the History of the Renaissance* in his first term. He never ceased quoting from the 'book which has had such a strange influence over my life', as *De Profundis* puts it. In an early poem, '*Humanitad*', Wilde's poetic 'I' aimed 'to burn with one clear flame', just as Pater notoriously instructed his readers in the closing pages of *The Renaissance*:

To burn always with this hard, gem-like flame, to maintain this ecstasy, is success in life. In a sense it might even be said that our failure is to form habits: for, after all, habit is relative to a stereotyped world, and meantime it is only the roughness of the eye that makes two persons, things, situations, seem alike. While all melts under our feet, we may well grasp at any exquisite passion, or any contribution to knowledge that seems by a lifted horizon to set the spirit free for a moment, or any stirring of the sense, strange dyes, strange colours, and curious odours, or work of the artist's hands, or the face of one's friend.

Wilde knew Pater's 'Conclusion' by heart. The author's subsequent suppression of it – in 1877 – only added to its preciousness.

Ruskin did not deign to take issue with Pater's ideas directly, but everything he argued for stood in opposition. His own defence of an aesthetic world view was rooted entirely in morality: the idea that artistic work was good for the individual and beneficial to society. Ruskin revered the Gothic arts – works founded in an age of faith. To Pater, the Gothic period was appreciated only insofar as it anticipated the greater, worldlier splendour of Renaissance culture. He appeared to celebrate moral ambiguity, and on occasion 'decadence'.

If Wilde's opinions would later closely shadow Pater's, he was nevertheless more obviously attracted by the character of Ruskin – in large part, as Pater was reclusive and aloof, whereas Ruskin got to know many of the brightest, most artistic undergraduates well. In June 1888, Oscar recalled their friendship: 'the dearest memories of my Oxford days are my walks and talks with you, and from you I learned nothing but what was good.' The two were intimates throughout. At least once, they went to the theatre together in London, to see Henry Irving play Shylock.

Earlier in the century, Newman's Oxford Movement had tried – and largely failed – to return the Church of England to its Catholic origins. Disaffected, Newman had converted in 1845, and would make a literary splash with a finely written defence of his reasoning, the *Apologia pro vita sua* (1866). Newman was no longer living in Oxford, but his example loomed large, and much of the crisis of faith that surrounded the Oxford Movement endured among undergraduates. Meanwhile, a small, as yet disorganised group of Roman Catholic students was finally permitted to study at Oxford. Wilde continued to ponder the relative merits of the faith he was brought up in, and the one he found more attractive and persuasive. At the end of his second year, he wrote to fellow student William Ward: 'About Newman, I think that his higher emotions revolted against Rome but that he was swept on by Logic to accept it as the only rational form of Christianity.' Oscar was sufficiently curious to buy 'a lot of [Newman's] books before leaving Oxford' that summer, 1876. One year on, he told Ward of plans to visit Newman in Birmingham, 'to burn my fingers a little more'; 'I am awfully keen for an interview, not of course to argue, but merely to be in the pleasure of that divine man.' It is unknown whether Oscar was invited, or went.

Oscar's father had been a Mason, and in his second term, Wilde himself joined the Apollo Lodge, dedicated exclusively to the university. Much of the costume – the velvet breeches, tail coat, white tie and silk hose – would later accompany him on his lecture tours. On first spying them, Bodley recorded, Oscar was 'struck by their gorgeousness'. At the after-induction dinner, his speech made joking reference to John the Baptist, whose life and especially death always had particular resonance, and would feature in *Salome*: 'I hope we shall emulate his life but not his death – I mean we ought to keep our heads.'

Wilde indulged himself rather too much in his first year. Like his mother, he took to entertaining regularly, providing gin and whisky punch and tobacco for anyone who cared to turn up on Sunday evenings. Organist Walter Parratt would play Wilde's own piano, accompanying a singer. It was not all idleness. Wilde's broad-based self-instruction meant that in Michaelmas – Christmas – Term of his first year, he never missed a lecture in the series given by Ruskin on Florentine art. An acquaintance recalled his 'large and flabby form'. Oscar was always 'conspicuous for something unusual in his dress, still more in his splendid head, his mass of black hair, his vivacious eyes, his poet's forehead, and a mouth like a shark's in formlessness and appetite.'

Ruskin exhorted the undergraduates at his lectures to abandon sport and help him complete something more socially useful. So it was that Wilde joined others in building a road bordered with flowers in Ferry Hinksey, west Oxford. This involved rising at dawn, and – Wilde later boasted – being permitted to fill 'Mr Ruskin's especial wheelbarrow'. Ruskin invited his cohort to breakfast after their exertions. As an undergraduate, Oscar was given to pronouncing in anti-industrialist, Ruskinian vein, as in: 'I would give Manchester back to the shepherds and Leeds to the stockfarmers.'

His end-of-first-term academic report – 'Responsions' – was predictably poor. Wilde rallied, however, when made to take a test in March 1875 – an unexceptional sanction – cramming by candlelight to get by. In June 1876, by contrast, he confidently took his first exams in Classics after two years' study. Wilde readily achieved a First Class result in 'Honour Mods', despite the upset of witnessing a further sharp decline in his father's health in Dublin the preceding Easter. Still, he did not bother to prepare for an accompanying paper in Divinity, which could be resat. An oral examination followed on 6th July. To Oscar's delight, it concentrated on his favourite, Aeschylus. He compared the Greek with Shakespeare and even a living poet Wilde revered and would soon meet in America, Walt Whitman. Oscar did not bother checking the 'list of honours' posted up after the exams, telling friends: 'I know I have a first. It's all a bore.'

Oscar took advantage of the long vacations to travel across Europe, a journey which was then cheap, and expected of Oxford undergraduates. Oscar toured Italy in the summer of 1875 – Ruskin's recommendations ringing in his ears – with Mahaffy and William Goulding, an Irish student. They followed a standard itinerary: Turin, Genoa, Florence, Bologna, Padua, Verona, Venice. What Wilde saw inspired much of his early verse, with its ongoing spiritual agonising. In 'At Verona' he adopted the poetic persona of Dante Alighieri, inspired by the poet's having being exiled there. Dante at first longs for death – 'better far / That I had died in the red ways of war' – but then rallies:

Nay peace: behind my prison's blinded bars
I do possess what none can take away
My love, and the glory of the stars.

Here, Oscar unwittingly prophesied his own time in exile, and indeed in prison too.

Correspondence home was more everyday. Titian's *Assumption* in Venice's I Frari church he commended to his father as 'the best painting in Italy'. He did not accompany the others to Rome, having run out of money. Instead Wilde wrote a poem, 'Rome Unvisited', which hinted strongly at his spiritual confusion:

O Roma, Roma, at thy feet,
I lay this barren gift of song!
For, ah! The way is steep and long
That leads unto thy holy street.

Wilde visited Paris on his way back to Ireland, next spending some weeks on the west coast there. Back in Oxford, he heard Cardinal Manning give a sermon at the dedication of St Aloysius, the first Roman Catholic church to open in the city for centuries.

The following year, on 19th April 1876, William Wilde died. His serious financial indebtedness was quickly exposed. Most of the family's properties were heavily mortgaged. What revenue there was even Wilde's mother would struggle to survive on. Illegitimate brother Henry died the next year. His will specifically disinherited Oscar from any monies emerging from his own father's properties, should he convert to Catholicism in the coming five years. In a letter of June 1877, Oscar duly complained to his peer Reginald Harding that his 'cousin' Henry had always been 'bigotedly intolerant' of Catholics, and 'seeing me "on the brink", struck me out of his will', as well as making the sanction against conversion: 'Fancy a man going before "God and the Eternal Silences" with his wretched Protestant prejudices and bigotry still clinging to him,' Wilde wrote with contempt.

Oscar's continued extravagance probably belied considerable financial anxieties. His long vacation after his father's death saw him in Dublin instead of Europe. In August 1876, he met the 'exquisitely pretty' Florence Balcombe. Three years Oscar's junior, she too was Anglo-Irish. The pair attended St Patrick's Cathedral together. That Christmas, he gave her a small gold cross. They dated after a fashion, though Wilde could hardly propose. (Balcombe would later marry Bram Stoker.) He was seen with other girls. At Oxford, meanwhile, he was developing a reputation for penning and encouraging unusually intimate correspondence with other male students. Bodley had noted in December 1875 that Oscar 'leaves foolish letters from people who are "hungry" for him'. One letter from his last year, addressed to a Balliol undergraduate, Harold Boulton, read: 'I wish music was not such a siren to you as to make you forget everybody else.' Oscar begged Boulton to meet him that evening, instead of another student 'whom by the bye I believe you like much better'. Around 1876, he started a highly suggestive, homoerotic poem, 'Choir Boy', never finished or published, concerning a 'man child lusty and fair / With little white limbs and little feet / A glory of golden yellow hair'.

Wilde was keen on talking about same-sex relations, then, if not on practising them. In an unguarded letter to William Ward of August 1876, Oscar referred to a mutual acquaintance, Todd, being seen at a Dublin theatre with 'young Ward the quire boy in a private box'. Wilde added:

Myself I believe Todd is extremely moral and only mentally spoons the boy, but I think he is foolish to go about with one, if he is bringing this boy about with him.

You are the only one I would tell about it, as you have a philosophical mind, *but don't tell anyone else about it like a good boy – it would do neither us nor Todd any good.*

Sensual expression between men – at Oxford and elsewhere – was increasingly explicit, yet also increasingly subject to attention and correction. A scandal in 1874 had involved a Balliol student called Hardinge, who had in his possession letters from Walter Pater signed: 'Yours lovingly'. When Benjamin Jowett, the college's Master, discovered this, he cut Pater off, summoned Hardinge – now known as 'the Balliol bugger' – and demanded he be sent down. He informed his father that Hardinge was 'living here in a way which might ultimately harm himself and was already throwing discredit on his college'. In 1876, Wilde sought out a visitor to Oxford, Oscar Browning, who had lately lost his teaching job at Eton because of his romantic attachment to pupils. Browning was a close friend of Pater's.

Wilde continued to flirt with Catholicism, and published some verse in expressly Roman magazines in Ireland. Like many undergraduates, he was preoccupied with the spiritual dilemma of whether to convert. At Balliol, Gerard Manley Hopkins had done so in 1866 – after reading Newman's *Apologia*. Wilde's friend David Hunter Blair did so in 1875, having stolen away to Rome to see the appointment as Cardinal of Henry Edward Manning, himself an Oxford convert. One visitor to Wilde's Magdalen rooms in 1876 spoke of their being filled with 'photographs of the Pope and of Cardinal Manning'.

Hunter Blair had his own property and was independent of his family, unlike Oscar. Wilde evinced sympathy, but could not follow suit. This was the first of three critical years in Wilde's religious crisis. His copy of Thomas à Kempis' *Imitation of Christ* dates from July 1876. Yet Oscar also sought solutions elsewhere, including in the Masons. He proceeded in November 1876 into the Apollo Rose-Croix Chapter, a new one, and very 'High Church'. In the arcane ceremony to 'take the eighteenth degree' Wilde was obliged to perform as Raphael. Catholics may not be Masons, and a letter to Ward of March 1877 suggests how Wilde was thinking of Freemasonry, paradoxically, as a sort of bulwark against his own conversion: 'I have got rather keen on

Masonry lately, and believe in it awfully – in fact would be awfully sorry to have to give it up in case I secede from the Protestant Heresy.' Still, he also attended St Aloysius and spoke of dreaming of Newman. He was not so much vacillating as oscillating between converting and not doing so: 'I shift with every breath of thought and am weaker and more self-deceiving than ever.'

Easter 1877 saw Wilde's first trip to Greece, again accompanying Mahaffy and a young Etonian student. His former tutor was determined to prevent Oscar from going to Rome literally or metaphorically: 'we cannot let you become a Catholic but we will make you a good pagan instead.' They went via Genoa and Ravenna down to Brindisi, the port for Greece. The route was fortuitous. When 'Ravenna' was announced later that year as the chosen subject for the university's Newdigate Prize for Poetry, Wilde had a distinct advantage.

Greece was charming. From Corfu and Zante, the three proceeded to Olympia, where they were granted a personal tour of the excavations. Athens impressed. They then detoured to Mycenae. By 21st April, Wilde was already over a fortnight late for term. Yet, against Mahaffy's wishes, he then sailed to Naples, delaying his return to join Hunter Blair and Ward in Rome. The former was determined to force the matter of his friend's conversion, and pulled off a coup – a private audience with Pius IX. This left Wilde dumbstruck with excitement. Afterwards, he wrote a poem, '*Urbs Sacra Aeterna*', which he sent directly to the Pontiff. Yet he did not convert. Indeed, to some he referred cheekily to Keats's grave as 'the holiest place in Rome'.

There was a last wobble. Just before Easter 1878 – a few months before finals – Oscar visited London's Brompton Oratory, confessed to Rev. Sebastien Bowden and prepared to enter the Catholic Church. Bowden wrote encouragingly, referring to Oscar's stated 'aimlessness and misery', 'your present unhappy self' and, more tangibly, to the 'bad influences mental and moral' that had compounded and corrupted Wilde's 'evil nature'. Bowden wrote of 'positive sin', implying that Oscar had spoken of sexual desires or even acts. Bowden urged Oscar to pray first, and then return for further counselling and confession in a few days. On the day he was due to enter the Church, Oscar did not show up, but instead sent the Oratory a bunch of lilies. Aestheticism would now be his only creed.

His extended travels abroad were not excused by Magdalen. Wilde was 'rusticated' – sent down – until October 1877, to take the academic year again. He later waxed indignant, telling Charles Ricketts, 'I was sent down from Oxford for being the first undergraduate to visit Olympia.' But the college was right. He had absconded during term for no good cause. A fine of £47 10s was levied, later halved on appeal.

Wilde first consoled himself in London. He heard Richard Wagner conduct *The Flying Dutchman*. On 30th April 1877, he caused a sensation at the opening of the Grosvenor Gallery by wearing a red coat shaped like a cello. As well as Pre-Raphaelite works, the gallery showcased paintings by the American Impressionist James McNeill Whistler, who would become Oscar's Chelsea neighbour and associate. Wilde reviewed the opening exhibition for the *Dublin University Magazine* favourably. His first critical writing, it was dear to him, for 'criticism is the highest form of autobiography', as Oscar later put it. His readership in mind, Wilde played the sceptical Irishman abroad, 'this dull land of England, with its short summer, its dreary rains and fogs, its mining districts, and factories, and vile deification of machinery, has yet produced very great masters of art'.

He sent the piece to Pater, whose reply of July 1877 praised the 'excellent article', 'you possess some beautiful and, for your age, quite exceptionally cultivated tastes: and a considerable knowledge too of many beautiful things.' Pater must have caught the innuendo in certain lines of Oscar's. He had discoursed on how 'in the Greek islands boys can be found as beautiful as the Charmides of Plato.' There were references to Guido Reni, Perugino and Correggio, all painters of sensual male youths, the last best capturing what Wilde termed 'the bloom and vitality and radiance of... adolescent beauty'.

The summer saw Wilde in Ireland. Finally, on his return to college in October 1877, he met Pater. They rapidly became close friends. Something more came from the encounter. Pater provoked Wilde by insisting that 'prose is so much more difficult' to write than verse. His acolyte picked up on the challenge, and determined to write more essays and reviews. Pater lent him Flaubert's recent *Trois Contes*, of which the secularised biblical narrative 'Herodias' was a key inspiration for *Salome*. They exchanged photographs, walked, took tea. Oscar Browning regularly visited Pater's Brasenose rooms. The gatherings were said to be attended by various 'feminine looking youths'. To be an intimate of Pater was already to invite scandal. Wilde chose to embrace it, writing many letters, now lost, to 'the great master'. Later, though he would always revere his prose, Wilde's view of Pater cooled. He was capable of scorn, even, telling Ricketts that Pater 'has lived to disprove everything he has written'. Max Beerbohm, on telling Wilde of Pater's death, was asked, 'Was he ever alive?'

Oscar was outgoing during his last Oxford year. For a May Ball in 1878, he hired a Prince Rupert costume with purple breeches. It was so fetching that he bought it. Wilde's biographer Richard Ellmann contends that he contracted syphilis around this time, and that it was diagnosed. But both this, and its putative source, a female prostitute, must be counted as conjecture. Some early biographies gave syphilis as the cause of Wilde's death, but likewise this may have been in error. Naturally, if Wilde knew he was syphilitic, this may well have contributed to his often doom-laden disposition (Ellmann's view), of which his wit was the natural flipside. If not, the temperament was real in any case.

Oscar worked enough to secure a top First in Finals, probably the best in the year. 'The dons are "astonied" beyond words – the Bad Boy doing so well in the end,' Wilde wrote to William Ward. He heard of his triumph following a viva, a month after an equally significant event – his public reading of the Newdigate Prize-winning poem 'Ravenna'. His mother wrote to praise her son, 'the Olympic Victor', on this triumph, characteristically seeing in his success echoes of her own gifts. Reflecting on the family's increasing impoverishment, she added, 'Well, after all, we have *Genius* – that is something attorneys can't take away.'

No offer of a fellowship was forthcoming. In any case, when challenged as to what he planned to do with his life, Oscar once replied, 'God knows. I won't be a dried-up Oxford don anyhow.' In the poem 'Humanitad', he associated scholarship with an unrealistic unworldly detachment: 'I cannot... live without desire, fear and pain... / Self-poised, self-centred, and self-comforted.' He accurately predicted the range of his future achievements instead, 'I'll be a poet, a writer, a dramatist. Somehow or other, I'll be famous, and if not famous, notorious.' Wilde added, 'These things are in the lap of the gods. What will be, will be.' Sanguine at being passed over by Oxford, Oscar, like Napoleon, saw fit to crown himself – not as Emperor, but 'professor of aesthetics and art critic', as he preferred. Wilde headed to London to pursue – as he termed it in a 'Confessional Album' at Magdalen – 'success – fame or even notoriety'. He would be granted all three.

Early Career: London, America and Beyond 1878–84

In the summer of 1878, Wilde returned to Ireland to oversee the sale of the properties he had inherited. Then he travelled to Oxford to retake a Divinity exam without which he could not graduate, finally taking his Bachelor of Arts on 28th November 1878. He got to know an aspiring undergraduate poet, Rennell Rodd, whom he toured around, introducing him to new friends such as James Abbott McNeill Whistler in London. Wilde moved to the city in December, but was initially unsure of his direction. He kept petitioning various parties in Oxford in case an academic post might be found, and formally applied and sat the exam for at least one fellowship.

From 1879, Oscar shared a flat with Frank Miles, a friend from Oxford and an artist – first in Salisbury Street off the Strand; later, in Tite Street, Chelsea. Wilde was introduced to many writers, artists, actors – and a stunning society beauty, Lillie Langtry, 'the loveliest woman in Europe'. Langtry was especially struck by Oscar's fine speaking voice, 'He had one of the most alluring voices that I have ever listened to, round and soft, and full of variety and expression.' The two were genuine soul-mates, and Oscar even instructed Langtry in Latin. It was rumoured that he carried a lily flower to present to its namesake every day. The conceit – true or not – resurfaced in Gilbert and Sullivan's *Patience* (1881).

Wilde cultivated appropriate friendships. He went to Folkestone in May 1879 to welcome the French actress Sarah Bernhardt to England, tossing an armful of flowers at her feet. Only Bernhardt and Ellen Terry could rival Langtry for Wilde's (non-sexual) affections. He not only encouraged Langtry to become an actress, he persuaded Henriette Labouchere, a retired actress, to coach her. Labouchere's husband Henry was the MP behind the Gross Offences act that would later see Wilde jailed.

Everywhere he went Wilde produced an apt turn of phrase, becoming a spokesman for aesthetic values. He was soon prominent enough to be suggestively lampooned in George du Maurier's *Punch* cartoons as the poet 'Maudle', for instance. One exchange, from 1881, has 'Maudle' discoursing 'On the Choice of a Profession':

> *Maudle*: How *consummately* lovely your son is, Mrs. Brown!
> *Mrs Brown* (a Philistine from the country): *What?* He's a *nice, manly* boy, if you mean that, Mr. Maudle. He has just left school you know, and wishes to be an artist.
> *Maudle*: Why should he be an artist?
> *Mrs Brown*: Well, he must be *something!*
> *Maudle*: Why should he *be* anything? Why not let him remain forever content to *exist beautifully?*
> [Mrs Brown determines that at all events her Son shall not study Art under Maudle.]

The cartoon summarises how the deliberate ambiguities in Wilde's aesthetic sophistry would be interpreted – not only by the 'Philistine' hordes but by society at large.

Wilde still spent much of his time in Oxford, literally and figuratively. In 1879 he submitted an essay on 'Historical Criticism in Antiquity' for the Chancellor's Essay Prize, for which graduates were eligible. His daring aesthetic argument proposed the contemporary age to be another Greek one, 'the age of style'. Probably Wilde's was the strongest submission, but unusually the examiners voted to withhold the prize, perhaps because of the piece's passing comments on the beauty of male youth.

On 3rd June 1880, at Oscar's suggestion, a production of Aeschylus' *Agamemnon* in Greek was performed in the hall of Balliol College. The extent of his involvement is unclear, but Wilde boasted that he had chosen the costumes, scenery and more. Rennell Rodd, who painted the scenery, had himself published a book of verse in 1880 entitled *Songs in the South*. In the summer of 1880, the pair travelled through the Loire valley together. Rodd always denied that their intimacy became sexual; it may not have done.

Wilde was afflicted by professional indecision. He suddenly decided to apply to become an inspector of schools – like a poet he admired, Matthew Arnold. He was unsuccessful – unsurprisingly, given the bizarre choice of Oscar Browning, sometime pederast at Eton, as referee. His mother, who moved to London with Willy in 1879, dreamt of a parliamentary career for Oscar. Meanwhile, he was fast spending the proceeds of the property sales. Bernhardt, whom he befriended, was a poor example, 'Money's meant to be spent,' she would exhort: 'Spend, spend it!' Wilde attended the triumphant first night of Bernhardt's London appearance as Racine's Phèdre on 2nd June 1879. He probably determined there and then to turn playwright. According to Ricketts, Oscar would nurture a lifelong wish to write a play about Queen Elizabeth, in which Bernhardt would star. He was similarly solicitous of Ellen Terry, in 1880 sending her a copy of *Vera, or the Nihilists*, his first play, which he had privately printed.

Vera reflected the sort of noble socialism which then appealed to Oscar. Still, he protested, it was a work 'not of politics but of passion'. If so, it would fail to set contemporary hearts alight. Wilde had prudently set *Vera* in the Russia of 1800. One consequence was that casual readers could not readily discern its relevance. As a study in the allure and danger of unfettered rebellion, *Vera* spoke volumes concerning Wilde's preoccupations with his own inclinations, including sexual ones. Dramatically, however, it was poorly structured. The London and New York producers whom Wilde sent it to turned it down.

Gilbert and Sullivan's operetta *Patience*, which opened on 23rd April 1881, was by no means the first attempt to lampoon aestheticism on the London stage, nor even the first vehicle in which an actor mimicked Wilde's expressiveness. Today, however, it is the only such satire to be even slightly known. Oscar was unmistakably the real-life inspiration for Bunthorne, its 'ultra-poetical, super aesthetical, / Out-of-the-way young man'. Wilde wrote to the actor playing Bunthorne before the show opened, requesting a seat at the opening night and 'looking forward to being greatly amused'.

He did indeed laugh at the debt to his own example. Bunthorne is said to walk down Piccadilly carrying 'a poppy or lily in his medieval hand'. Wilde later drew attention to the exaggeration involved here, commenting in America in 1882 that 'to have done it was nothing, but to make people think one had done it was a triumph'. Inevitably, he and W.S. Gilbert the librettist met – at a supper party. Oscar shone. Gilbert commented, 'I wish I could talk like you. I'd keep my mouth shut and claim it as a virtue!' Wilde artfully responded, 'Ah that would be selfish! I could deny myself the pleasure of talking, but not to others the pleasure of listening.'

His literary career was launched in 1881 with *Poems*, half of the sixty-one pieces of which were previously unpublished. Oscar used David Bogue, the same house that had published Rodd. It was virtually a private undertaking, since Wilde underwrote the printing costs. An initial run of 750 copies was agreed, using hand-made paper from Holland. Demand was high, and throughout 1882, two further printings ensued. *Poems* also came out through an American house. Wilde designed a title page provocatively featuring a papal tiara poised over a Masonic rose; both were encircled by an oval. In the poems likewise, Wilde flirted with Catholicism, paganism, ecumenical Christianity and Masonic tradition. Their hallmark was a sort of inconstancy of mood. Indeed, Wilde commented afterwards that 'my next book may be a perfect contradiction of my first'.

He received cautious praise from Arnold, Swinburne, John Addington Symonds and, naturally, Rennell Rodd ('brilliant writing'). Reviewers were uncharitable. Some accused him of indecency; others of not outraging enough. *Punch* argued, 'The poet is Wilde, / But his poetry's tame.' The Oxford Union asked for a copy for its library. However, a debate on the matter ensued, in which the author's supposed literary thefts were itemised. A motion was passed not to accept the volume, and it was returned. Wilde accepted the rebuke generously, though his letter expressed the 'regret... that there should still be at Oxford such a large number of young men who are ready to accept their own ignorance as an index, and their own conceit as a criterion of any imaginative and beautiful work'.

One poem received particular attention, 'Charmides'. This picked up on Pater's study of Winckelmann in *The Renaissance*, which spoke of the German classicist's fond touching of ancient statuary. Wilde connected the image to a story told by Lucian of a man who fell in love with a statue. Wilde's figure, Charmides, lusts after the virginal figure of Athena:

And then his lips in hungering delight
Fed on her lips, and round the towered neck
He flung his arms, nor cared at all his passion's will to check.

As in *Dorian Gray*, Wilde flaunted such profane desire only to have it punished; Athena persuades Charmides to drown himself. Frank Miles' father, a canon, wrote to his son, however, asking him to leave Wilde, given this poem's scandalous nature. He then wrote directly to Wilde, asking for a 'separation for a time' from his son, 'because you do not see the risk we see in a published poem that makes all who read it say to themselves, "this is outside the pale of poetry", "it is licentious and may do great harm to any soul that reads it."' To Wilde's distress, Frank Miles, dependent financially, was forced to agree that they part. Wilde packed, but promised, 'I will never speak to you again as long as I live.' He took lodgings at 9 Charles Street, off Grosvenor Square.

Meanwhile, *Patience* had become a huge hit, conferring infamy upon Wilde. In June 1881, the Prince of Wales requested an audience, a self-consciously witty inversion of protocol, 'I do not know Mr Wilde, and not to know Mr Wilde is not to be known.' He was invited to a séance – then very much the fashion – at Tite Street, and was charmed by both Wilde and Miles. The show's producer, Richard D'Oyly Carte, saw a further opportunity after the show's transfer to New York, and invited Wilde to give a series of lectures there upon aesthetic topics. Wilde would doubtless have preferred to see *Vera* taken up by one of the leading figures in the theatrical world. He needed money, however, so accepted the D'Oyly Carte offer, setting sail for New York on Christmas Eve 1881 to instruct the New World in 'The English Renaissance of Art'.

Wilde had a special set of clothes made, booked elocution lessons, and then took to the itinerant life immediately. The original, brief schedule would be extended repeatedly in response to public demand. It would finally last almost a year, spanning the States and Canada too. Wilde's endurance necessitated the drumming up of two variant lectures. In 'The Decorative Arts', he argued that bad wallpaper might justifiably cause a youth to turn to crime. 'The House Beautiful' corrected myriad vulgar tendencies in design. Each was duly recorded and circulated by the British, American and European presses. In London, Wilde's adventures would ultimately be viewed ambivalently. Yet before he embarked Henry Labouchere was typical when he opined in *Truth*: 'The Americans are far more curious than we are to gaze at all those whose names, from one cause or another, have become household words... Mr Wilde... has a distinct individuality, and, therefore, I should fancy that his lectures will attract any who will listen and look.'

Oscar achieved celebrity the moment the SS *Arizona* docked on the evening of 2nd January 1882. He cleared quarantine the following morning, but canny American journalists chartered a launch to the ship in order to capture firsthand the sayings of London's famous wit. Wilde seemed unconcerned at the fact that the actual lecture – which he had long pondered and had planned to tackle on board – lay unwritten. Oscar was sketched, photographed and quoted relentlessly. He may or may not have told the New York customs officer, 'I have nothing to declare except my genius.' It scarcely matters, the epigram fitted the occasion so well. On ship, he certainly remarked on his disappointment at the timid Atlantic, 'The roaring ocean does not roar.' *Truth* duly printed a letter from 'The Atlantic Ocean', which began, 'I am disappointed in Mr Oscar Wilde.'

In New York, Wilde attended *Patience*, commenting when Bunthorne came on stage dressed as himself, 'This is one of the compliments that mediocrity pays to those who are not mediocre.' He tried hard to persuade someone to produce *Vera*. He also secured a private meeting in Camden, New Jersey with America's appointed 'national poet', Walt Whitman. Then sixty-three, Whitman was author of *Leaves of Grass*, whose 'pantheism' Wilde celebrated, calling it 'Greek'. He told Whitman that his mother had read from his verse in his childhood, and that he had carried *Leaves of Grass* around on his Oxford walks.

Whitman offered the 'fine handsome youngster' home-made elderberry wine, drilling him about Swinburne. He gave Wilde a photograph to convey to Swinburne, and another for himself. They did not entirely agree over the course of some three hours, but Wilde afterwards proclaimed an 'admiration for that man which I can hardly express'. Whitman's character was 'the closest approach to the Greek we have yet had in modern times'. They met again in May 1882. Wilde is claimed to have reported afterwards, 'The kiss of Walt Whitman is still on my lips.'

Later in Washington, he would less successfully meet Henry James, whose fiction he had praised. James mentioned missing London. Oscar misjudged the moment as an opportunity for

levity, 'Really? You care for places? The world is my home.'
James was furious, later referring to Wilde as 'a fatuous fool'. A
meeting with poet Henry Wadsworth Longfellow, who had
corresponded with Oscar's mother, was more successful. There
were other less high-brow entertainments. Wilde was fleeced by
gambling criminals in New York – he wrote plaintively that he
had 'fallen into a den of thieves'. Later he would make the same
thing happen to Dorian Gray.

Oscar first lectured on 9th January 1882 at New York's
Chickering Hall. Receipts were $1211, a huge sum even for a
sell-out. The only precedent was Charles Dickens' tour of the
continent, where he had performed the very scene of Little
Nell's death which Wilde later ridiculed. He was conscious of
the precedent, writing to England that 'the hall had an audience
larger and more wonderful than even Dickens had'. Wilde
sported a full-length green coat, dandyish clothes, much of it
drawn from his Masonic regalia, with velvet and silk predomin-
ating. His flowing, feminine locks of hair, pallid complexion,
unworldly poise and ready wit were celebrated and ridiculed
in turn. The *Boston Evening Transcript* asked, 'Is he manne, or
woman, or childe?' In the Rocky Mountains, notoriously, Oscar
descended into Leadville Silver Mine to instruct its employees
in the life beautiful. For this lecture, Wilde made particular
mention of Cellini casting his bronze statue of Perseus. A new
shaft was named 'The Oscar' in honour. He ate supper with the
miners, which consisted of nothing but whisky, he claimed.

What he normally said on tour was surprisingly unexceptional, and went down well with audiences. He saw in the
English Renaissance 'a sort of new birth of the spirit of man'.
The spiel had just the sort of idealistic tenor to appeal to listen-
ers versed in the positivist spirituality of American Renaissance
authors like Emerson and Thoreau. Wilde's final sentence was
delicately Paterian, and delivered with an affectation of Pater's,
the faux-colloquial 'Well': 'We spend our days looking for the
secret of life. Well, the secret of life is art.'

Not all were won over. *Harpers Weekly* of 28th January featured an illustration of the lecturer as 'The Aesthetic Monkey', adoring a sunflower. Wilde was pressed by Irish-Americans as to why he was promoting an 'English Renaissance' when Britain participated in the 'hideous tyranny' of what they considered occupation. These words were part of a headline in the New York paper *Irish Nation*'s coverage of the visit by 'Speranza's Son'. Oscar cleverly reiterated his ancestry, and prophesied a culturally resurgent Ireland too. In May 1882, nationalist terrorists murdered the new Chief Secretary for Ireland and his Under-Secretary as they crossed Phoenix Park. Wilde told an American journalist that England was 'reaping the fruit of seven centuries of injustice'. Charles Stuart Parnell, leader of the Home Rule Party, was imprisoned. Wilde declared himself a 'thorough republican'.

The *New York Tribune* took against the speaker they called 'the penny Ruskin'. The *Washington Post* was another enemy. Wilde told *The New York Times*, however, that he welcomed negative comment, 'If you survive yellow journalism, you need not be afraid of yellow fever.' More perturbing was the habit of local students turning up at several venues, dressed in high aesthetic garb, including sunflowers in their hats, to ridicule Wilde's message. This began at Harvard. Wilde parried well, but at other venues the students interrupted and booed him.

As notices worsened, publicly Wilde stayed stoical. Of his critics, he told one journalist, 'They have certainly treated me outrageously, but I am not the one who is injured, it is the public. By such ridiculous attacks, the people are taught to mock where they should reverence.' He cited exiles such as Shelley, who, he said, had written as well in Italy as England. He visited a prison in Lincoln, Nebraska, where Wilde illustrated his faith in the popular 'science' of physiognomical profiling – that is, judging people's moral disposition by way of their features. He commented on the 'dreadful face' of one inmate. (His concern that immorality might not be written in one's appearance informed the plot of *Dorian Gray*.) Another was 'a beast, an animal'. Afterwards, he wrote, 'They were all mean looking, which consoled me, for I should hate to see a criminal with a noble face.' Wilde made a flippant joke of one prisoner who read sensational fiction, 'My heart was turned by the eyes of the doomed man, but if he reads [Charlotte Yonge's] *The Heir of Redclyffe*, it's perhaps as well to let the law take its course.' Another inmate had Shelley and Dante on his shelves, which Wilde found inexpressibly poignant. (Later, after spending time in prison himself – where he too read *The Divine Comedy* – he would effectively atone, conferring nobility upon the prisoner awaiting execution in *The Ballad of Reading Gaol*.)

Financially, he did very well out of the lecture tour. 'They all say you are making heaps of money, and I smile and accept the notion – for it galls the Londoners,' his mother wrote. Wilde did not worry that his earnings rather contradicted his message: that love of the beautiful was vital to 'temper and counteract the sordid materialism of the age'. It was one of many contradictions he would enjoy and embody. Likewise, his radicalism was tempered in respect of the Irish question when he spoke in the more conservative South: 'I do not wish to see the empire dismembered, but only to see the Irish people free, and Ireland still as a willing and integral part of the British Empire.'

He stayed on in New York for two months after the tour's end. Lillie Langtry was in town, but the chief reason for delay was a bout of malaria. Wilde also discussed with one impresario the possibility that his second, then-unfinished play, the period drama, *The Duchess of Padua*, be performed. In fact, the same producer found it easier to cast *Vera*, which would open in 1883.

Oscar returned to London briefly before immersing himself in Parisian artistic circles from January 1883. He did find time to meet Whistler and Rodd, by now close friends. Wilde had arranged to have Rodd's volume, *Rose Leaf and Apple Leaf*, published in America, adding a preface, which his friend did not like. It cast Rodd very much as Wilde's follower, one of 'many young men' in his 'modern romantic school'. It also spoke of their holidays together. When published in November 1882, the volume was met with ridicule. In February, Rodd would end his acquaintance with Wilde, who felt aggrieved that his intervention was not appreciated. Rodd became 'the true poet, and the false friend'. He was the first of many.

In Paris, Oscar was welcomed by Paul Verlaine, Victor Hugo and Edmond Goncourt among other writers. Goncourt had written a decadent novel, *La Faustin*, about an actress partly based on Sarah Bernhardt (whom Wilde also saw perform). *La Faustin* later supplied the Sibyl Vane subplot in *Dorian Gray*. In his journals, Goncourt showed his dislike of the Irishman 'of dubious sex, with the speech of an inferior actor, telling tall tales'. Wilde met painters too, such as Jacques-Emile Blanche the famous portraitist, and Impressionists Pissarro and De Nittis. Not everybody was warm. Edgar Degas told Walter Sickert that Wilde struck him as 'playing Lord Byron in a suburban theatre'.

A young Englishman befriended him. Robert Harborough Sherard would later become Wilde's first biographer. Twenty-one, athletic and blond, he was also William Wordsworth's great-grandson. Sherard dedicated a collection of poems, *Whispers*, to Wilde, after attracting his attention at a dinner party. As Oscar held forth on the Venus de Milo, Sherard interjected that 'the Louvre' always made him think of the shopping gallery opposite where he bought his ties; he had never been in the museum itself. Wilde found this 'pose' irresistible, took Sherard out for dinner, and insisted they use first names, 'You mustn't call me Wilde. If we are only strangers, I am Mr Wilde'. He became, as he desired, Oscar instead.

In Paris, Wilde embraced fashionable theories of anarchism, such as Pierre-Joseph Prudhon's famous maxim, 'Property is theft'. Possibly this was also a tribute to Sherard, so impressed by the French Revolution that he still used its calendar on his letters. Wilde coined him 'Citoyen Robert Sherard.' They discussed marriage, which appealed to Sherard. Wilde, who would in fact marry first, warned him that women were always unfaithful. He himself visited a female prostitute at least once, exclaiming afterwards, 'What animals we all are, Robert.' Wilde was taken with Sherard's looks, praising what he felt was 'the head of a Roman emperor of the decadence'. Oscar then reinvented himself, by way of a severe bowl haircut in the style – he claimed – of Nero. To achieve this, he escorted a hairdresser to the Louvre to show him a bust – perhaps of Nero, perhaps of Hadrian's lover Antinous.

Wilde also changed his clothing, donning a black overcoat, a gesture of ascetic restraint after his American outfits. Sherard had not liked the ostentatious look, and praised the reinvention. The Irishman insisted: 'We are now concerned with the Oscar Wilde of the second period, who has nothing whatever in common with the gentleman who wore long hair and carried a sunflower down Piccadilly.' He reported on returning to London that '[n]obody recognizes me and everybody tells me I look young.' The startling change reflected a need to cast off his recent incarnation as lecturer. It also marked a determination to advance his literary career. Wilde claimed to be working hard in Paris, once telling Sherard he had proofread a poem all morning 'and took out a comma'. In the afternoon, he had continued to work, putting the comma back again. He worked on a new poem, 'The Sphinx', and completed *The Duchess of Padua*, only to hear that the American actress he had wanted to see in the main role had turned it down.

In May 1883, Wilde returned to London. He was keen to renew his acquaintance with one Constance Lloyd, daughter of a London lawyer. For the previous few years, despite his American earnings, Oscar had had constant money worries. The right marriage might solve them – and answer nascent gossip concerning his sexual character. *Punch* had recently called him, unambiguously, a 'Mary-Ann'. Wilde had self-consciously flirted with several women between 1880 and 1884, and had proposed at least once – to Charlotte Montefiore. Her rejection provoked the famous riposte, 'I am so sorry about your decision. With your money and my brain we could have gone far.'

Oscar first met Constance in May 1881, and was especially struck by her ability to read Dante in Italian. She was fluent in French, and after their marriage, learnt German at his request. Constance was timid, yet a good conversationalist when relaxed. She was naturally bright. Wilde told his mother after their first meeting, 'By the by, Mama, I think of marrying that girl.' He must have appreciated her companionship considerably, describing her to Lillie Langtry as 'a grave, slight, violet-eyed Artemis, with... wonderful ivory hands'. Wilde was not given to praising women's appearance, other than that of actresses, but he valued Constance's slight, boyish looks. Later in Paris, Wilde would object to the very idea of feminine attractiveness, 'Women aren't beautiful at all. They are something else, I allow: magnificent, when dressed with taste and covered with jewels, but beautiful, no. Beauty reflects the soul.' Still, he was beguiled by Constance's quietness above all, 'She scarcely ever speaks, and I am always wondering what her thoughts are like.' Ricketts quoted Wilde as stating that 'women would be wonderful if they had not been taught to speak.'

An understated courtship resumed immediately on his return. Constance liked Oscar, but for a somewhat worrying reason, 'because when he's talking to me alone, he's never a bit affected, and speaks naturally'. Oscar had another side of his character which he would keep for family, but it would never eclipse his theatrical manner and self-publicising instincts. Sexually, any match with a woman could hardly turn out well, as Oscar must at least by now have suspected. He longed, though, in part, for conventional approval. The prospect of a marriage, naturally, pleased his mother more than anyone.

To earn money, Wilde arranged a long lecture tour around the British Isles, starting in July at the Royal Academy. His friend Whistler gave much advice, and would later take credit for most of what Oscar said. On 10th July, the tour proper began at

Prince's Hall, Piccadilly. The lecture offered Wilde's 'Impressions of America'. It was mostly knockabout stuff. Wilde waxed lyrical on the 'melancholy place' Niagara Falls, 'filled with melancholy people who wandered about trying to get up that feeling of sublimity which the guide books assured them they could do without extra charge'. He joked about his Mormon audience in Salt Lake City, the wives gathered in doughnut shape around their husband. Asked if the theatre there was big enough, he had replied, 'Oh, yes, it will hold nine families.' He made the odd serious point, noting that pirate editions of his *Poems* had been on sale. The two countries did not have a copyright agreement, and non-American authors were invariably ripped off. He joked that the natives were far too animated, 'I only saw one reposeful American – a wooden figure outside a tobacco shop.'

Henry Labouchere attended the talk, and dropped his earlier enthusiasm for Wilde. His organ, *Truth*, carried a leader headed, 'Exit Oscar', noting that '[n]o one laughed at him more than he laughed at himself.' The 'effeminate phrase-maker' had lectured to a half-empty hall, it claimed. Wilde tartly commented that '[i]f it took Labouchere three columns to prove that I was forgotten, then there is no difference between fame and obscurity.' For now, that was that, but Labouchere was to have a more direct, and unexpected, impact on Oscar's future.

After touring the provinces, Wilde boarded the SS *Britannic* on 2nd August 1883. His first venture into playwriting was to be tested on 20th August at New York's Union Square Theatre. Wilde had plenty of suggestions for the producer and star, Marie Prescott, even carrying some vermilion cloth over for the production. *Vera* opened to a full house, there was applause, and Wilde made a short speech at the end of the third act. It was a very hot evening, however, which exacerbated the fact that – to Americans especially – the story of Russian 'nihilists' was largely incomprehensible. One paper pronounced it 'really marvelous'; the rest were dismissive. The *New York Times* critic wrote ostentatiously, 'We do not doubt the sincerity of Mr Oscar Wilde, who, nevertheless, has given us cogent reason to doubt his sincerity.' Though the piece contained 'cleverness and wit', in toto it was 'as near failure as an ingenious and able writer can bring it'. Marie Prescott's performance was criticised too. She defended it, and the 'noble' play, but it closed on the 28th in response to poor takings. Prescott was compelled to move it to Detroit.

Wilde returned to England, unusually reserved. There were more lectures, starting in Wandsworth on 24th September 1883. Between engagements, he pursued Constance Lloyd with increasing ardour. They found themselves both in Dublin by November, where Wilde lectured on 'The House Beautiful'. (Yeats, aged eighteen, recalled attending.) On the 25th Oscar proposed, and Constance accepted. Much of their romantic correspondence has not survived, though we do have Constance's acknowledgment of Wilde's presumably general admission of previous intimacies: 'I am content to let the past be buried, it does not belong to me.' Unfortunate with hindsight was her pledge that 'when I have you for my husband, I will hold you fast with chains of love'. Wilde would indeed feel constrained – 'bored to death with the married life' – in due course.

Lloyd's grandfather supported the nuptials, but asked Wilde about a difficult matter: debt. Wilde finessed the situation, and continued to tour, since receipts were helping to reduce his borrowings. Constance was granted the sum of £5000 in advance from her grandfather's estate, to be held in trust, with interest on the capital providing a living income. She had a further £250 a year to live on, and upon her grandfather's death, this would rise to £800. He helpfully expired in July the following year.

Whistler threw the couple an engagement party in December. Lady Wilde was thrilled, and once more predicted a political career. Willy professed himself delighted, toasting 'Alcibiades and Lady Constance.' The allusion was unwittingly poignant, since although this Ancient Greek politician and general was known as 'Prince of talkers', his loyalties were also questioned, and even his sexuality. Oscar and Constance were not married for a further six months – on 29th May 1884 at St James's Church. The groom himself designed Constance's cream-coloured satin dress, and equally elaborate ones for the bridesmaids. Their honeymoon in Paris involved artistic explorations. With Constance, Wilde again saw Sarah Bernhardt as Lady Macbeth, and Whistler's new works at the Salon. The pair were invited to dinner by another fashionable American artist, John Singer Sargent. Wilde abandoned his bride at one point, too, taking a long walk with young Sherard. Wilde steered conversation toward a bawdy account of his deflowering of Constance. The frankness made Sherard uncomfortable.

Before the Wildes headed back, Oscar gave a long interview to the *Morning News*, published on 20th June 1884, in which he expounded upon a recent novel he admired: Joris-Karl Huysmans's *À Rebours* (in English, *Against Nature* or *Against the Grain*) was the scandalous hit of Paris. It concerned only one character – the indolent, spoilt, degenerate Des Esseintes – whose dissolute behaviour includes encrusting his pet tortoise's shell with jewels, only for it to be crushed by the weight. Though he would have other models in mind, such as Pater's *Renaissance*, Wilde later admitted in court that Huysmans's work was the 'poisonous French novel' that Dorian Gray felt, peculiarly, 'contained the story of his own life, written before he had lived it'. In Wilde's novel, the book is never named, though he originally gave it a fictitious title, *Le Secret de Raoul* by 'Catulle Sarrazin'. Still, the thrill of recognition which Gray experienced surely replicated Wilde's own in 1884. It related to a number of semi-veiled allusions in *À Rebours* to Des Esseintes's sexual liaisons – with young boys as well as women.

Middle Career: London
1884–91

Wilde had fame, a wife, and a new four-storey home at 16 Tite Street. He had this decorated by the celebrated E.W. Goodwin, the 'greatest aesthete of them all' according to Beerbohm. Whistler refused the commission: since Wilde had lectured on 'The House Beautiful', he must now deliver. Wilde did so – but at huge expense. The couple began borrowing – at first, £1000 from Constance's grandfather's capital. The redecoration was protracted too. After their honeymoon, the Wildes were forced to live with friends, relatives or in hotels. The works went on for seven months. Among the ostentatious Art Nouveau designs and fittings, which betrayed a heavily Japonist influence, there was a Moorish-styled library on the ground floor, with no chairs, but a divan. Wilde invariably wrote here, though he originally also had a study on the third floor, which became the boys' bedroom. Constance and Oscar had separate bedrooms on the second.

In January 1885, they finally moved in. Cyril, their first son, was born there on 5th June 1885, and Vyvyan followed on 5th November 1886 – an inauspicious date for Catholics, Wilde thought, despite not being Catholic. It was formally recorded as the 3rd. If his career as writer was pretty much stillborn, Wilde was now writing anonymously for the *Pall Mall Gazette*, the *Dramatic Review* and other outlets. He was still a celebrity. To make ends meet, in late 1884 he agreed to yet another British lecture tour, with new topics such as 'The Value of Art in Modern Life' and 'Dress'.

In 'Dress', Wilde argued that clothes should be hung from the shoulders, not the waist, as they had been in Ancient Greece. The other lecture conspicuously praised Whistler as someone who 'had rejected all literary titles for his pictures' – the titles reflected only the 'tone' of the canvases. But Oscar's prominence disagreed with Whistler, notwithstanding this praise. The artist felt Wilde had plagiarised his own ideas. At the absurd hour of 10p.m. on 20th February 1885, Whistler dispensed his 'Ten O'Clock lecture', denouncing an unnamed but readily identifiable 'unattached writer' who only presumed to represent good taste.

Whistler argued that Wilde had demonstrated a 'complete misunderstanding' of the aesthetic principles he and others stood for. Wilde's theory of artistic self-improvement he particularly disputed. Art was not only about beauty, but about finding beauty in the unattractive. The next day, Wilde countered in print that 'the arts are made for life, and not life for the arts'. He and Whistler jousted in the press a while, Oscar initially misinterpreting the attack from his friend as only sport. Still, he insisted in his responses that the supreme artist was not the painter, but the poet. He reiterated his view that Whistler was 'one of the very greatest masters of painting... And I may add that in this opinion Mr Whistler himself entirely concurs.' A year later, Whistler sought to have Wilde removed from a committee dedicated to reform in the arts, arguing brutally, 'What has Oscar in common with Art? Except that he dines at our tables and picks from our platters the plums for the pudding he peddles in the provinces.'

Lecturing and dinner invitations kept Wilde away from Constance. Frank Harris first mentioned Wilde's repugnance at her pregnant form – 'heavy, shapeless, deformed', he is supposed to have said. Oscar may never have expressed himself so directly, but it is likely that Constance's pregnancy exacerbated his growing dislike of women's bodily shape. Oscar had always idealised the athletic male form, and began forming many close attachments with young men. These may not have been sexual, but certainly involved explicit, often disarming, sensual appreciation and expression. Robert Sherard had become Oscar's intimate in Paris. Harry Marillier, an undergraduate at Peterhouse, invited him to Cambridge to see a production of the *Eumenides* in November 1885. Wilde forced a swifter meeting in London, afterwards telling Marillier how 'intensely dramatic and immensely psychological' their hour together had been. In Symonds and elsewhere, 'psychological' was used as a code for same-sex affections. By such words, homosexual men recognised one another. Wilde once informed Richard Le Gallienne, 'I can recognise a whole life in the choice of an adjective.'

After the Cambridge visit, where he entertained a group of boys, Wilde wrote less guardedly. Marillier had 'the love of things impossible… *l'amour de l'impossible* (how do men name it?)' This was a reference to the medieval, theological conception of sodomy as an unnamable crime among Christians. This idea later blossomed as Alfred Douglas' 'love that dare not speak its name'. Wilde continued recklessly: 'I myself would sacrifice everything for a new experience.' He offered the boy visions of a sensual Arcadia, 'an unknown land full of strange flowers and subtle perfumes… a land where all things are perfect and poisonous'.

The Greek model of close male male relationships was summarised in Plato's *Republic* by Socrates, who explicitly argued against their sexual expression. A younger man's beauty might be strongly appreciated by an elder. He was to be given gifts, educated, encouraged into maturity. The younger man was to admire the intelligence and example of his lover. Notwithstanding Socrates' chaste views, Ancient Greek culture had allowed such closeness to tip over into physical expression – according to certain protocols, and for a finite period, that is, until the boy's sexual maturation. Introducing these principles of 'Greek love' into the context of Victorian patriarchal culture was to be Oscar Wilde's biggest challenge, and ultimate undoing. Though he spoke in code, he did not insist on this love's idealised, non-sensual character – quite the reverse.

Constance was pregnant with Vyvyan when Oscar first met Robbie Ross in 1886. Son of a Canadian Attorney-General, Ross, seventeen, was not classically good-looking, at least by the standards of Wilde's other infatuations. He had, Oscar claimed, 'the face of Puck', and was squat and boyish. He and Wilde became close over the eighteen months before he went up to King's College, Cambridge. Ross is often said to have been the first to initiate Wilde into sexual acts; both parties claimed this. However, Wilde had good reason to have it understood that he had been faithful to Constance earlier – during the courtship and her first pregnancy. It is simply unknown whether Wilde truly had not succumbed earlier. Nor is it clear what sort of sexual initiation took place.

Wilde was thirty-three. Ross was certainly forward for his age – indeed for *the* age. He 'came out' as homosexual to his mother at eighteen, which was simply unheard of. Ross would suffer at Cambridge for his flamboyant aestheticism, leaving without taking his degree. He remained important to Wilde, even after their sexual relations ceased. He was there when Wilde died, oversaw his burial and looked after his literary reputation in the following years, falling out with Douglas in consequence. Wilde nicknamed him 'St Robert of Phillimore' – after the gardens in London where Ross's family lived. Robbie was also a devout Catholic.

The Wildes stopped having sex following Vyvyan's birth. This was common in Victorian England, especially for couples wanting to stop having children. Constance was reassured overall by Oscar's occasional kindness, and his attentiveness towards his children. Wilde was a natural storyteller, and the tales he devised for his sons would later find successful publication as *The Happy Prince and Other Tales* (1888) and *A House of Pomegranates* (1891). He was compared to Hans Christian Andersen. The volumes, if mannered, were widely praised and sold well. Constance certainly did not initially suspect anything untoward in his friendships with younger men.

Wilde's income between 1886 and 1889 was considerably boosted by the distinctive and amusing book reviews he wrote. He always thought of them as only journalism, setting them aside when he was able to. Meanwhile, the need for regular income was irresistible. In an unlikely move, Wilde negotiated to become editor of a new magazine, *The Lady's World*. He took charge in May 1887, slowly adjusting the content to make it less 'feminine' and more 'womanly' (his words). For the first issue in November he secured the publisher's agreement to change the condescending title. The pink front cover announced the arrival of '*The Woman's World*, Edited by Oscar Wilde'. After the triumphant reception of this issue, he lost interest, especially in the day-to-day aspects of running a magazine. Wilde turned up at the office increasingly rarely, and did not always write his own column. He found space for a piece on 'Irish Peasant Tales' by his mother, and for two pieces by Constance. Wilde resigned from the editorship in October 1889.

The relationship between his personal sexual liberation and the urge to write something more serious was central to Wilde. Ross inspired him to start 'The Portrait of Mr W.H.' in late 1887, though it was not published until July 1889. This was originally an essay in which Wilde argued that Shakespeare's genius had arisen from his love for a boy-actor in his company. (Around this time, Wilde began comparing his own profile to Shakespeare's.) 'Will Hughes' was seventeen, the age at which Robbie began his affair with Oscar. A letter to Ross concedes 'the story is half yours, and but for you it would not have been written'.

The piece was reworked after Frank Harris persuaded Wilde that it was drastically indiscreet. Others advised suppression. It became, instead, a complex fiction, in which an unnamed narrator is told by a friend, Erskine, that someone called Cyril Graham holds such views concerning Shakespeare. The beloved boy was said to have had his name planted subtly within his poems. Wilde himself toyed with the story's straddling of fiction and non-fiction, telling Helena Sickert, 'You must believe in

Willy Hughes. I almost do myself.' Even after revision, 'The Portrait of Mr W.H.' was potent. It can be interpreted as Wilde's first overtly dangerous publication. As Harris commented, 'it gave his enemies for the first time the very weapon they wanted.' Wilde expanded the magazine version, making it bolder still, but the publisher Elkin Mathews refused to take it on 'at any price'.

Ross was indelibly present in *The Picture of Dorian Gray*, although it was Oscar's next infatuation – John Gray – who would give his surname to Wilde's most famous creation. Gray was something new. Born on 10th March 1866 of humble stock, he had effectively improved himself since leaving school aged thirteen. When he and Oscar met, Gray was working as a clerk in the Post Office. He would later be promoted to a clerkship in the Foreign Office Library. Gray had been taken up by an aesthetic group surrounding two male artists who lived together in 'The Vale' in Chelsea, Charles Shannon and Charles Ricketts. Wilde had first been in touch with Ricketts to commission a portrait of Willy Hughes in autumn 1889. In August, Gray had an article published in Shannon and Ricketts' new magazine *The Dial*. Wilde asked to be introduced to the young man, and a sexual relationship probably followed – one which would involve setting Robbie Ross gently aside. Wilde helped Gray's literary career, and the borrowing of his name for his novel has been seen as an act of seduction. Gray acknowledged the fact, once signing himself 'Dorian' in a letter to Oscar. (Wilde took the name 'Dorian' from one of the more prominent Ancient Greek tribes.)

Wilde also underwrote the publication of a volume of Gray's poems, *Silverpoints*, paying for the book's design by Ricketts and Shannon. By the time of *Dorian Gray*'s publication in book form in 1891, Gray was twenty-five. Lionel Johnson, a poet at Oxford who was taken up by Wilde around the same time, reported, however, that Gray retained 'the face of fifteen'. The notion of someone of enchanting beauty failing to age was central to Wilde's novelistic storyline, so the deployment of Gray's surname was entirely apt. John Gray was in Oscar's shadow for a good while, characterised by George Bernard Shaw as 'one of the more abject of Wilde's disciples'.

The often assumed sexual nature of the Wilde–Gray relationship is open to some doubt. In *De Profundis,* Wilde contrasted the carnality of his encounters with Bosie, and their shared appetite for boys, with the more cerebral union he had experienced with other youths, including Gray. Likewise, Wilde may or may not have had sex at New College, Oxford with Lionel Johnson in February 1890. The boy told a friend unguardedly after their first meeting, 'I am in love with him.' Numerous other youths were brought on by Wilde, including John Barlas, a crazed poet, also of New College, who thought himself a biblical character. There was André Raffalovich, a young French writer who had settled in London and who would later take up with Gray. Oscar initially found that, though unattractive, Raffalovich had 'the right measure of romance and cynicism'. They soon fell out, and the Frenchman's recollections of Wilde are ungenerous. By 1890, he had written *A Willing Exile*, a hostile fictional version of the Wilde circle, and of Oscar's marriage to Constance – they appear as 'Cyprian and Daisy Broome'.

There was Richard Le Gallienne, whom Oscar met in 1888, a handsome young poet who revelled in the attention. He seems to have distanced himself by the time Oscar wrote plaintively two years later, 'I hope the laurels are not too thick across your brow for me to kiss your eyelids.' Bernard Berenson, later a famous art critic, did not allow intimacy. 'You are made of stone.' Oscar told him. The author Max Beerbohm was an unusual adoptee in Wilde's entourage, as he always behaved older than he actually was.

Meanwhile, one of Wilde's last book reviews shows his growing embrace of socialist ideas. He was responding to a collection of working-class folk songs gathered by Edward Carpenter, whose *Towards Democracy* (1883) was a set of Whitmanesque political poems Wilde must have seen. Carpenter would go on to proselytise for homosexuality before, during and – bravely –

after Oscar's fall. Wilde's drift from an idealistic anarchism towards socialism would be clearly announced in a brilliant article of 1891, 'The Soul of Man under Socialism'. He wrote fast throughout this period, and it saw the publication of a number of important non-fictional pieces which would consolidate his critical thinking – 'The Truth of Masks', 'The Decay of Lying' (Wilde's fullest summary of his views concerning the relationship between life and art), 'Pen, Pencil and Poison', about forger Thomas Wainewright, and 'The Critic as Artist'.

In 1891, the four essays were published together as *Intentions*. (Wilde's short stories, too, were individually well received, reappearing in a book, *Lord Arthur Savile's Crime and Other Stories*, the same year.) Wilde made a number of coded comments in these. Of Wainewright, he argued that the criminal displayed 'that curious love of green, which in individuals is always a sign of a subtle artistic temperament, and in nations is said to denote a laxity, if not a decadence, of morals'. A love of green was, in short, symptomatic of homosexuality – this informed Wilde's adoption of the symbolic green carnation later.

But by now, Oscar's literary fame rested on another, even more suggestive work: *The Picture of Dorian Gray*. The novel first appeared in its entirety in *Lippincott's* magazine on 20th June 1890. The arrangement came out of a dinner on 30th August 1889, offered by J.M. Stoddard, the publisher of *Lippincott's*, to Wilde and Arthur Conan Doyle. Stoddard wanted more strong literary fiction, commissioning on the spot both Conan Doyle's tale 'The Sign of Four' and *Dorian Gray*. He asked Wilde for 100,000 words. Wilde prevaricated, missed a few deadlines, and told Stoddard: 'There are not 100,000 beautiful words in the English language.' He was nervous about the endeavour, describing early parts of the book as 'all conversation and no action'. However, his mother thought *Dorian Gray* 'the most wonderful piece of writing in all the fiction of the day'. Still, it immediately caused scandal. Constance reported how suddenly 'no one will speak to us.'

The novel's storyline involves a subtly eroticised triangle of relationships between three men. It has numerous plausible sources, though one rarely discussed may have constituted Wilde's reading matter as he wrote it. *Noodlot* (1890), the second novel by the Dutch author Louis Couperus, appeared in English in 1891 as *Footsteps of Fate*, though it is more properly translated as *Fate* or *Destiny*. Wilde is known to have admired it, and probably came upon it well before the English edition came out, being a friend of the translator, Alexander Teixera de Mattos. In *Noodlot*, Bertie, an effeminate, dandyish figure, is shown exploiting his straightforward, but corruptible friend Frank. When Frank announces plans to marry Eve, Bertie is vexed to madness, and is determined to manipulate the situation so that the wedding does not happen. When Bertie succeeds in this, by faking a letter, Frank kills him, and goes to jail for the crime. He and Eve marry, but the relationship is cursed. The novel ends by their committing suicide together. *Noodlot* took a decadent theme, but described it naturalistically. Though Wilde's own prose was very different, he took note of the provocative representation of Bertie's longings, which went much farther than in peer works.

Two other sources are Wilde's own ancestor Charles Maturin's *Melmoth the Wanderer* (1820), in which a young man discovers the portrait of an evil relative in an attic, and, most obviously, Huysmans's non-novelistic novel *À Rebours*. Huysmans's elaborate descriptions of Des Esseintes's lavish lifestyle, interiors, reading matter, preferences in music, art and the like were joined by endless and repetitive outbursts on the subject of his own malaise, moral experimentation and degeneracy, his cultural isolation, social superiority and romantic follies with women and young boys. Des Esseintes endures syphilis, and its equally awful treatments. *À Rebours* had a wide impact in England even before its appearance in translation. Arthur Symons called it the 'breviary of the Decadence'. To one correspondent, Wilde wrote in April 1892 that *Dorian Gray* was 'a fantastic variation on Huysmans's over-realistic study of the artistic temperament in our inartistic age'.

If *Dorian Gray* has a claim to be the only 'Symbolist' novel written in English (though Symbolism is a notoriously difficult movement to define), it can also be said to be an effective transposition of Huysmans's intentions in the French work into the context of literary London. Huysmans had himself only distilled the decadent sensual and sexual transgressions long suggested in French verse – by Verlaine, Rimbaud, Mallarmé, Lautréamont and Baudelaire. But there was something more toxic in the depiction of a willing degenerate in narrative form. With his next novel, *Là-Bas* (1891; in English, *Down There*), Huysmans trumped the shock value of *À Rebours*, depicting the voguish prevalence in Paris of Satanism, the occult, black masses and orgies.

Concerning other sources for *Dorian Gray*, Ellmann noted the possible influence of Henry James' *The Tragic Muse* (1890). In this work, Gabriel Nash, an aesthete, has Wildean inflections. He sits for a portrait, but leaves, bored, before it can be finished. The incomplete Nash on canvas soon fades away. Robert Louis Stevenson's novella *Dr Jekyll and Mr Hyde*, an instant hit on publication in 1886, may also have inspired Wilde's handling of the 'double' presence of corrupted Gray and uncorrupted portrait. We know of the book's significance for Wilde. He had 'Vivian' tell 'Cyril' in his Socratic essay 'The Decay of Lying' (1889) that Stevenson's realism left him culpable; he had been caught 'robbing a story of its reality by trying to make it too true'. 'Vivian' later returns to *Jekyll and Hyde*, 'this curious psychological study of transformation' to insist on the inevitability of life imitating art.

Wilde's peers not only pursued the literary influences on *Dorian Gray*. They equally demanded real-life models. The author was suitably contradictory on this question. An early biographer, Hesketh Pearson, told of Wilde's being painted by one 'Basil Ward' in 1884. Wilde spotted another sitter, a beautiful youth, exclaiming to the artist, 'What a pity that such a glorious creature should ever grow old!' The artist agreed,

'How delightful it would be if he could remain exactly as he is, while the portrait aged and withered in his stead!' But no artist of this name has been traced. In September 1890, the *St James's Gazette* reported how when, three years earlier, Wilde's portrait was being painted by a Canadian, Frances Richards, Oscar suddenly commented, 'What a tragic thing it is. This portrait will never grow older, and I shall. If it was only the other way.' Ernest Dowson argued in a letter of October 1890 that it was known that Charles Shannon had been Wilde's 'prototype' for Basil Hallward. Wilde played with his enquirers, however, telling one, 'Basil Hallward is what I think I am: Lord Henry what the world thinks me: Dorian is what I would like to be in other ages, perhaps.' In Reading prison, he was asked, 'What are you doing in this place, Dorian Gray?' and replied, 'Not Dorian Gray, but Lord Henry Wootton.'

Of *Dorian Gray*'s representation of aestheticism, it is a commonplace to state that Wilde showed the tragic impossibility of living by artistic creeds alone. Perversely, however, for its publication in book form, Oscar tacked on the pure, aestheticist dogma of its preface: 'There is no such thing as a moral or an immoral book. Books are well written, or badly written. That is all.' Yet the novel sees Dorian and Basil punished. If art's aim was to escape biographical reading – 'to conceal the artist', as the preface has it – *Dorian Gray* fails, since both Basil and Dorian trigger their own destruction by fearing what they read in, or into, the portrait. Likewise, Lord Henry Wootton's insistence to Dorian that one cannot be 'poisoned by a book', since 'art... annihilates the desire to act', can be read not so much as wish-fulfilment, but rather as a deliberate deception.

The deployment of *Dorian Gray* in court would leave Wilde reiterating Wootton-type pronouncements, but the efficacy of its example as used by his opponents underlined the folly of Lord Henry's arguments. They assumed an individual's invulnerability in respect of others' views, a position Wilde flirted with, but was to have challenged. Equally, the flirtation was inconsistent. Responding to hostile reviews, Wilde argued perversely that he now found *Dorian Gray* too moral: it taught how 'all excess as well as all renunciation, brings its own punishment'. The author of one particularly hostile piece in the *St James's Gazette* was visited by Wilde in person. Oscar told Samuel Jeyes revealingly that he stood by the novel, 'I mean every word I have said, and everything at which I have hinted in *Dorian Gray*.' 'Then,' retorted Jeyes, 'you are very likely to find yourself at Bow Street [police station] one of these days.' Another revealing comment came from Wilde's letter to Ada Leverson of July 1893, some three years after its publication: 'It is quite tragic for me to think how completely he [Dorian Gray] has been understood on all sides!' Wilde neither wrote, nor meant, 'misunderstood'.

The extent to which *Dorian Gray* discussed homosexuality is a vexed topic. Even Huysmans described Des Esseintes's attraction to street boys covertly. Still, to some degree Wilde deliberately transgressed by introducing 'Greek love' into his own book. Ellmann cleverly mentions a sentence in 'The Soul of Man under Socialism': 'Any attempt to extend the subject-matter of art is extremely distasteful to the public; and yet the vitality and progress of art depend in a large measure on the continual extension of the subject-matter.' Typically, in court Wilde sought to have it both ways. The sentiments expressed towards young male beauty in his writings came, he argued, out of a long, noble historical tradition. They only appeared to augur something new. His novel similarly argued: 'It was such love as Michael Angelo had known, and Montaigne, and Winckelmann, and Shakespeare himself.'

The innuendo in *Dorian Gray* was, however, deafening – for those inclined to hear. The impact of Dorian's face upon Basil's art is compared to that of Antinous upon Hadrian, his lover. Wilde's hero models himself on dissolute, polysexual Roman Emperor Heliogabalus. In April 1891, Wilde's second choice of publisher brought his novel out in book form. Macmillan, first approached, declined the novel. Wilde had added chapters, and deleted a sentence that became pivotal in the trials. W.H. Smith refused to sell the 'dirty' work. From this time on, Wilde's literary reputation would always have scandal attached to it.

That July, or thereabouts – there is contradictory evidence – a second-year undergraduate, blond, fair-skinned and standing at around 5ft 9in, was introduced to Wilde by Lionel Johnson. The effect was immediate and electric. Douglas had devoured *Dorian Gray* at Magdalen, and adored it and its author. Sometime lover of Wilde, himself a poet and Oxford undergraduate, Johnson soon found himself nudged aside. Lord Alfred Douglas – known to his friends as 'Bosie' – became Wilde's new obsession. He was Oscar's one real love.

Late Career: London, Paris and Beyond 1891–5

Wilde attended the literary salon of Stéphane Mallarmé in February 1891. The revered Symbolist poet was critical in Wilde's decision to write a major work in French, especially as that work would concern the same subject – Salome – as a famously unfinished poem by Mallarmé himself, 'Hérodiade'. Both were fans of Edgar Allan Poe, and after a successful first meeting, Mallarmé sent Oscar his translation of Poe's 'The Raven'. In early November, Wilde returned to Paris, this time to stay two months. Sending a copy of *Dorian Gray* to 'the master', he asked Mallarmé if he could attend the next salon – on 3rd November. One difficulty was that Whistler, to whom Wilde had not spoken for years, frequently attended. The American missed no opportunity to malign his former friend. This time, writing to tell Mallarmé he would not be attending on the 3rd, Whistler added that it was unfortunate that he therefore could not 'denounce' Oscar. He instead sent a telegram to arrive just before Wilde himself: 'Precaution: Familiarity Fatal; Hide the Pearls'.

Wilde's arrival in Parisian society was otherwise acclaimed. He was introduced to Marcel Proust by the portraitist Jacques-Emile Blanche. Marcel Schwob, another young writer, was infatuated with Wilde's writings, but disappointed in the man, with his 'large pasty face, red cheeks... bad, protruding teeth, [and]... vicious, childlike mouth'. Wilde boasted to Schwob of consorting with 'bandits, murderers, [and] thieves'. If unattractive, however, Wilde was undoubtedly fascinating. Schwob, like others such as Pierre Louÿs and André Gide, was captivated. Gide, at twenty-two fifteen years Oscar's junior, was obsessed. He and Wilde met each day for several weeks. Gide initially confided to his diary his total admiration for Wilde. A month later, however, the young Protestant felt his soul had somehow been endangered. By January 1892, he could write that the acquaintance with Wilde 'did me nothing but harm... I lost the habit of thinking.' Gide would later write a memoir of Wilde, and also fictionalise him as the dissolute 'Ménalque' in *Les Nourritures terrestres* (1897; *Fruits of the Earth*).

Gide grew so perturbed at the impact Wilde had had on him that he later removed from his journals all entries relating to the first weeks of their friendship. We can never know what was said or proposed to unsettle him so, but it surely related to sexual ethics. Wilde was clearly acting, and talking, provocatively. Leon Daudet thought him treacherous; the Irishman wrote to him insisting he was 'just like a tiny, tiny child'. Paul Valéry did not believe in Wilde's play of innocence, describing him as a 'symbolic mouth *à la* [Odilon] Redon which swallows a mouthful and mechanically transforms it at once into a satanic aphorism'.

The Biblical story of Salome had been treated by many writers and artists in the nineteenth century. It appealed to the Romantic temperament of the age, for it allowed the representation of unfettered female desires. Heinrich Heine and Flaubert had used it before Mallarmé. Flaubert's story in turn inspired Jules Massenet's 1881 opera *Hérodiade*. In 1888, Wilde had reviewed a narrative poem entitled 'Salome', written by an American, J.C. Heywood. The decadent-Symbolist artist Gustave Moreau had painted several representations of the 'heroine', two of which had in turn been rhapsodically described in Huysmans's *À Rebours*.

By late 1891, Wilde was obsessed by the possibilities offered by Salome's character – particularly of sensual excess. According to Ross, he often talked of her portrayal in art, 'Don't you think she would be better naked? Yes, totally naked, but draped with heavy and ringing necklaces made of jewels of every colour, warm with the fervor of her amber flesh.' Wilde was drawn by the idea of shocking the public, and perhaps also by the possibility of projecting his own, unsanctionable sexual instincts onto the wanton female, 'Her lust must needs be infinite, and her perversity without limits.' The story's ending required Salome to be punished for her erotic pursuit of John the Baptist. But *Dorian Gray* had already illustrated how a narrative could both underline moral norms and remain somehow ambivalent about the aesthetic, sensual priorities its lapsed heroes espoused. Nor was Salome the only character to be punished. In Wilde's version, Herod would likewise stand condemned of inappropriately lusting after his own daughter.

Wilde took to the idea of putting his *femme fatale* on stage. Transgressiveness drove him. He cited approvingly the example of Florentine artist Cellini, who was said to have 'crucified a living man to study the play of muscles in his death agony'. Wilde argued that the Pope had been correct to absolve Cellini, 'What is the death of a vague individual if it enables an immortal word to blossom and to create, in Keats's words, an eternal source of ecstasy?' His Salome would not carry John's head meekly to her mother, Herodias. She would order it for herself out of thwarted passion and kiss the dead man on the mouth, if he would not allow the kiss when alive. Wilde had already settled on his chosen actress – it could only be Sarah Bernhardt.

He returned to London shortly before Christmas in 1891 to finish *Salome*, hoping that it might be staged quickly in Paris or London. A problem was that Wilde the dramatist still was not bankable. In January 1891, he had seen his second full-length drama, *The Duchess of Padua*, staged in New York, though it was retitled *Guido Ferranti*. It had not even been credited to Wilde, so as not to connect it to *Vera*'s earlier failure. It was praised by the critics, one of whom unmasked its author in a generous piece for the *New York Tribune*, which regretted only a 'radical defect of the work... insincerity'. This very quality Wilde would have to deploy on stage in a different manner before he would achieve success.

Guido Ferranti ran for just three weeks. Initially Oscar had expectations that – as *The Duchess of Padua* – it would next be performed in London. He offered it to actor-manager George Alexander, who had been appointed to run the St James's Theatre in 1890. Alexander, however, asked for a contemporary work instead. In summer 1890, he commissioned a society drama to open the theatre's first season the next year. Wilde procrastinated, and in February 1891 offered to return his advance. Alexander refused the offer, and, though it came in over a year late, accepted Wilde's first comedy, *Lady Windermere's Fan*, under the provisional title 'A Good Woman'. Wilde had worked on the manuscript intermittently over eighteen months, but struggled with the new genre. After just a few days with his family over New Year holidays, he took off for Torquay to polish it and *Salome*.

Wilde attended the rehearsals of *Lady Windermere's Fan* daily, arguing animatedly with Alexander over many details. It was worth it. The first night – on 20th February 1892 – was a triumph. Wilde had cause to be doubly thrilled. His determination to pursue a dramatic career had been vindicated. He had also shown commercial acumen. When Alexander offered a thousand pounds for the 'simply wonderful' play, Wilde refused the money, settling instead for a percentage. This earned him several thousand pounds in the first year of performance alone. The author was called to the stage, and, while smoking, delivered an acclaimed and much reported speech, 'Ladies and gentlemen: I have enjoyed this evening immensely. The actors have given us a charming rendition of a delightful play, and your appreciation has been most intelligent. I congratulate you on the great success of your performance, which persuades me that you think almost as highly of the play as I do myself.' He wore a green carnation, as did one character, Cecil Graham. Wilde also asked a coterie of young men – Ross, the artist Graham Robertson and others – to do likewise. The carnations, artificially dyed, were code for unnaturalness of a different sort. But when Robertson asked what it meant, Wilde shrewdly replied, 'Nothing whatever, but that is just what nobody will guess.' In 1894, Robert Hichens would publish a satiric novel about Wilde and the cult of aestheticism entitled *The Green Carnation*.

Another character, Lord Darlington, was first in a line of Wilde's creations to betray a belief in aesthetic values but to produce the sort of paradoxical statement which would undermine them. In *Lady Windermere's Fan*'s opening act, Wilde's heroine professes herself disappointed at the 'elaborate compliments' Darlington has paid her. Lady Windermere begs Darlington to assure her of his insincerity, since 'I like you very much... But I shouldn't like you at all if I thought you were what most other men are.' In Wilde's stage-play world, deceit was encouraged, even rewarded.

Not all present were enthusiastic: Henry James thought it 'infantine... both in subject and form'. But *Lady Windermere's Fan* remained a hit, running till 29th July, then touring, and reopening in town on 31st October. Suddenly Wilde the dramatist was in demand. *A Woman of No Importance*, *An Ideal Husband* and *The Importance of Being Earnest* would refine the formula, which some critics noted had a debt to the author of French melodramas, Victorien Sardou. Wilde claimed to revere few living dramatists. The Norwegian Henrik Ibsen appealed for his willingness to shock bourgeois audiences, but his example was too wedded to a 'realist' presentation of circumstance and character. Wilde had, of course, borrowed – but from further back in the English theatrical tradition: from Restoration comedies by Congreve, Wycherley and Sheridan. But he had also brilliantly updated the archetype.

Sarah Bernhardt was understandably thrilled at the idea that she play the lead in a new play by the dramatist of the moment. By June 1892, rehearsals were underway for a London run of

Salome. Graham Robertson was asked to design the production, and manufactured an extravagant golden dress 'sustained on the shoulders by bands of gilt and painted leather which also held in place a golden breastplate set with jewels'. Bernhardt was to wear a triple crown atop flowing blue hair. Two weeks in, however, it became known that the Lord Chamberlain, licenser of all theatrical performances, was considering banning *Salome*. According to the then law, no biblical figure might be represented on stage. Wilde took his case to the press, 'If the censor refuses *Salome*, I shall leave England to settle in France where I shall take out letters of naturalization. I will not consent to call myself a citizen of a country that shows such narrowness in artistic judgment. I am not English. I am Irish, which is quite another thing.'

He may even have been serious. To a French journalist, he lamented the 'anti-artistic and narrow-minded' English, 'There is a great deal of hypocrisy in England which you in France very justly find fault with. The typical Briton is Tartuffe, seated in his shop behind the counter. There are numerous exceptions, but they only prove the rule.' The British press reacted with humour, noting that as a Frenchman, Wilde would be conscripted.

Oscar resolved at the least to publish his unperformable play. He first enlisted Louÿs, Schwob and others to finesse his French. *Salome* was co-published in Paris and London in a luxurious purple edition with silver type in February 1893. Wilde circulated copies throughout literary London and Paris, and was especially thrilled at Mallarmé's approval of 'the inexpressible and the Dream' in it. Maurice Maeterlinck, the Belgian Symbolist playwright whose work *Salome* most closely resembled, found it 'mysterious, strange and admirable'. Wilde now longed for an English language edition, with illustrations. He had already spotted a drawing of Salome holding John the Baptist's head in an edition of *Studio* magazine. Wilde sought out Aubrey Beardsley, a young, truculent artist responsible for this work, and immediately commissioned him. Beardsley's extraordinarily lavish illustrations for *Salome* made his name overnight. Wilde professed them 'quite wonderful', though he may have resented the attention they received. The text of the play in translation was a more awkward matter. Wilde allowed his beloved Bosie to undertake it. It was an indulgence, and a rare professional mistake.

Oscar was exhausted. In July 1892, he took a rest cure in Bad Homburg – probably with Bosie. He was made to diet and to stop smoking, however. The recuperation was too unpleasant to be a success. On his return, Wilde rented a farm near Cromer, Norfolk to concentrate on his next play, *A Woman of No Importance*, which he had promised to Herbert Beerbohm Tree, impresario and actor at the Haymarket Theatre. This time, Bosie was certainly around. Constance and the boys awaited him in Torquay. But Wilde told his wife he could not join them because Douglas had fallen ill. Constance suspected nothing, even offering to visit Cromer to help their young friend recuperate.

Wilde submitted the play in October. Though it has dated less well than his other comedies and is structurally weak – 'epigrams engulf it like the sea', noted Lytton Strachey – *A Woman of No Importance* retains some charm. Tree was delighted, especially with its dandyish anti-hero, Lord Illingworth, whom he would play. The playwright told Tree that Illingworth was 'certainly not natural... [but] a figure of art. Indeed, if you can bear the truth, he is MYSELF.' Illingworth was given a succession of choice epigrams, such as 'The English country gentleman galloping after a fox – the unspeakable in full pursuit of the uneatable'. An innovation was that Wilde provided him with a rhetorical sparring partner in Mrs Allonby.

Again, Wilde frequented all rehearsals. Tree was asked if the author had assisted the production, and replied that he had put it on 'with the interference of Wilde'. *A Woman of No Importance* opened on 19th April 1893 and was another hit. Beerbohm reported a mixed reception at the first night, however: 'When little Oscar came on to make his bow there was a slight mingling of hoots and hisses.' This time, when Wilde took to the stage, he did not make a speech; with his next plays, he chose not to take a curtain call. He could afford to wait for the critical verdict, which was generally positive. *The Times*, formerly hostile, found the play 'fresh in ideas and execution'. Wilde's commercial prospects were now very strong. He later recalled that at the height of *A Woman of No Importance*'s popularity, he had been earning '£170 to nearly £200 a week'.

From this time on, Oscar saw Constance and his boys less often. He did his writing from rented addresses or hotels, usually with Bosie in tow. Their relationship had become intense. It remains unclear when exactly it began. Wilde claimed he had hardly known Douglas until early in 1892, when he was asked to help the boy out financially, a worrying augury, as Bosie was being blackmailed over a love letter. Wilde secured the services of his own lawyer, George Lewis, who paid the extorter £100 to clear up the matter. Oscar then stayed a weekend in Bosie's rooms in Oxford. By June 1892, he was smitten. His inscription to Bosie in a copy of *Poems* he gave him that month reads:

From Oscar
To the Gilt-mailed
Boy
at Oxford
in the heart
of June
　　　　　– Oscar Wilde.

He wrote to Ross of how Bosie 'lies like a hyacinth on the sofa, and I worship him'. Douglas was 'quite like a narcissus – so white and gold'. Indulgent as the sentiment of the letter is, it indicated how Bosie was capable of diverting Wilde from his work. Paradoxically, as Douglas made Wilde less productive, he felt inspired to write verse himself. Between late 1892 and 1894, Bosie wrote many decent poems, characterised by a mixture of coyness and intimacy. The first, ironically, was entitled 'De Profundis'. Another, 'Two Loves', celebrated as its poetical 'I' 'the love that dare not speak its name'.

At other times, Bosie's temperamental volatility upset Wilde, preventing work in another way. Douglas was emotionally unstable all his life. Like his father, he was prone to imagining or exaggerating slights. He may simply have inherited something approaching insanity, generic to the Queensberry men, and more than evident in his father's later conduct. Beerbohm thought Bosie 'obviously mad'. Still, Wilde loved Douglas obsessively. Like all obsessive passions, this one was relentless, blind and finally destructive.

Later in life, from a variety of perspectives, Bosie would repeatedly recast the relationship. It is generally agreed that some content and much of the emphasis of *Oscar Wilde and Myself* (1914), *Autobiography* (1929) and *Without Apology* (1938) is misleading. Douglas invariably cast himself after Wilde's death as sexually innocent – in part understandably, given public morality and the legal position, but also disingenuously, given society's assumptions concerning age-differential relationships. However, the evidence – the early blackmailing, and Douglas' proselytising for homosexual rights when Wilde was in prison – points another way. Just as Ross probably inducted Wilde sexually, it is likely that Bosie only furthered Oscar's exploration and interest.

Douglas was already experienced. He admitted that at his own school, Winchester, 'the practice of Greek love is so general that it is only those who are physically unattractive that are reduced to living without love'. He was first repelled by the 'sink of iniquity', but grew to 'enjoy' its 'immorality', and left school 'ripe for any kind of wickedness'. He subsequently told Harris, however, that when Wilde first seduced him in Tite Street, he did in fact introduce Bosie to a new sexual possibility – fellatio. It was Oscar's preferred form of intercourse. Bosie's father Queensberry was blunt on the matter, saying of Wilde,

'That man is a cock sucker.' His son always insisted on one thing regarding his own sexual nature: he was never anally penetrated: 'I must be explicit: sodomy never took place between us, nor was it thought or dreamt of.'

Douglas' mature erotic interest was with boys, especially those of working- or lower-class origin. Oscar grew to share this interest – to the point of becoming enslaved by it. Spending time with rent-boys, pimps and blackmailers he later – in *De Profundis* – called 'feasting with panthers'. The 'panthers' hung around music halls, parks, along Piccadilly or at The Crown pub in Charing Cross, almost additional forms of entertainment. The threat of extortion was a major part of their appeal for Wilde.

In preparation for rehearsals of *A Woman of No Importance*, the pair had taken rooms in the Savoy Hotel. As the hit drama played throughout 1893, Wilde and Douglas spent time with their usual circle. But they had also begun using Alfred Taylor, a public school-educated small-time pimp, to meet young 'renters', perhaps as early as autumn 1892. The first boy Taylor procured for Oscar was probably Sidney Mavor. The next, Freddy Atkins, was a first-class blackmailer at seventeen. Not all Wilde's assignations were with prostitutes, though a financial element might still creep in. He was also conducting an affair with a handsome but psychologically unstable publishing clerk, Edward Shelley, who would later testify against him in court. Wilde had cause to be especially bitter at the treachery, having repeatedly agreed to Shelley's many requests for money over the course of a year.

In February 1893, Douglas sent on to Wilde a seventeen-year-old called Alfred Wood. They did not so much share this boy as use him alternately. Wilde had Wood stay with him in Tite Street in his wife's absence. On one occasion, Bosie gave the boy clothes, foolishly unaware that several compromising letters from Wilde were in a pocket. One that we know was among them responded to a poem of Bosie's:

My Own Boy, Your sonnet is quite lovely, and it is a marvel that those red rose-leaf lips of yours should have been made no less for music of song than for madness of kisses. Your slim gilt soul walks between passion and poetry. I know Hyacinthus, whom Apollo loved so madly, was you in Greek days…

> – Always, with undying love, yours, Oscar.

Wood wanted to finance a new start in America, and seized this opportunity for blackmail. In April, he waited for Wilde at the stage door of the Haymarket, demanding £60 for the letters' return. When Wilde refused, Wood decided to give the letters back anyway – except for this, the most damaging one. Wilde weakened at the apparent generosity and gave Wood £30.

Willie Wilde referred to Oscar's being surrounded by 'a gang of parasites'. Other intimate friends were repelled by Oscar's drinking and indulgence of youths quite unlike him in class or manner. John Gray, for one, experienced a gradual estrangement, which coincided with his being courted by André Raffalovich. By March 1893, Gray had broken with Wilde. This may also have been caused by the anonymous publication of an original and distinctive piece of gay erotic fiction, *Teleny, or the Reverse of the Medal*.

Almost everything we might suspect about this curious work remains conjecture. It was evidently written by not one but several people, sometime in the early 1890s. If the account of bookseller Charles Hirsch is to be believed, Wilde, who first left the manuscript of *Teleny* with him, was involved either in bringing contributors together, or – more probably – contributed at least one substantial section, and oversaw or edited the rest. There are passages that resemble *Salome*, and references to many of Wilde's favourite writers: Dante, Chaucer, Shakespeare, Shelley, Symonds. There may even be a punning clue in publisher Leonard Smithers' announcement of the book – available at the extortionate price of five guineas, in a limited run of just

200 copies. *Teleny* is described as 'a most extraordinary story of passion; and while dealing with scenes which surpass in freedom the *wildest* licence, the culture of its author's style adds an additional piquancy and spice to the narration' (my italics).

Both Ross and Gray have been suggested as fellow contributors, though many of Wilde's friends might have been involved. Still, if Gray had not consented to *Teleny*'s publication, and now feared being linked to it, this would be strong grounds for cutting Wilde off. Gray never wrote down his reasons for the break, telling Pierre Louÿs, 'It will suffice that I recount its origins when I see you in London.'

In April 1893, Louÿs attended the opening of *A Woman of No Importance* at Wilde's invitation, but wrote dismissively to his brother of the boys gathered around the playwright. Still, when asked to compose a French sonnet based on the dangerous 'Hyacinth' letter – which Wood had copied out to show Wilde, but kept – Louÿs, himself heterosexual, agreed. The poem appeared in the Oxford magazine *The Spirit Lamp*, which Douglas himself edited, in May 1893. Louÿs' patience was finite, however, and after a scene at the Albemarle Hotel – where Bosie and Oscar were then staying – he resolved to give up the friendship. Constance had brought her husband his post from Chelsea, and was begging him to return to Tite Street. Wilde merely joked to Louÿs, 'I've made three marriages in my life, one with a woman and two with men!' In May 1893, Louÿs visited Wilde in Paris, urging him to break with Bosie and to consider his family. When Oscar refused, Louÿs informed him of his decision. Wilde saw him out, saying only: 'I had hoped for a friend; from now on I will have only lovers.'

In May, Wilde also visited Douglas at Oxford. It was only a month before Bosie's finals, which he refused to prepare for. Attempts to have him privately tutored had been futile. Bosie resolved not to bother sitting the exams, and had his name removed from Magdalen's college records – to his father Queensberry's fury. The summer found the pair idling in 'a most unhealthy and delightful' house in Goring-on-Thames, as Wilde called it. They invited a few guests, even including young Cyril Wilde, aged eight. Douglas brought some undergraduates to stay, which evidently displeased Oscar, who was working hard on *An Ideal Husband*. After a furious argument, Wilde told Douglas they must separate, 'An irrevocable parting, a complete separation is the one wise, philosophic thing to do,' he announced grandly. Bosie left for London, but in three days was penitent, begging to be allowed back. Wilde struggled to find something to occupy his lover.

Translating *Salome* for its English edition seemed ideal. But Douglas simply wasn't up to it. He showed Wilde a manuscript littered with elementary errors. In inflammatory exchanges, Douglas childishly insisted that any errors lay in the original. Wilde reiterated the need to finish their 'fatal friendship'. Douglas weakened, and, with someone's intercession, won Oscar over with reassurances of his love. By September, writing from France, where he was resting alone, Wilde had tacitly taken Bosie back. Still, he insisted on changes to *Salome*, which Douglas stubbornly informed the publisher he could not allow, 'as I cannot consent to having my work altered and edited, and thus to become a mere machine for doing the rough work of translation, I have decided to relinquish the affair altogether.' He suggested Wilde translate himself. Beardsley even provided his own version. Oscar finally agreed on a compromise text, merely correcting Bosie's worst errors. Douglas settled for a dedication as translator, instead of a full credit. Peace, incredibly, was restored. Douglas wrote to the publisher that the resolution had left him 'persuaded that the dedication which is to be made is of infinitely greater artistic & literary value, than the appearance of my name on the title-page'. He was persuading himself, comparing it to 'the difference between a tribute of admiration from an artist and a receipt from a tradesman'.

The first of several scandals hit in October 1893. The father of Claude Dansey, a sixteen-year-old 'schoolboy with wonderful eyes' – Oscar's words – threatened to sue. The boy had been passed on sexually from Ross to Douglas to Wilde in just three days, and then told his parents. Ross and Douglas travelled to Belgium to meet the headmaster of the boy's school. They returned all letters and offered a settlement, and Wilde, naturally, paid. It was an incredibly lucky escape from which Oscar might have learnt, for all three could well have been prosecuted. Dansey senior decided not to proceed when he was informed that his son might also face jail.

On such occasions, Oscar both indulged and repented. Constance still implored him to return to Tite Street. His mother's letters also had an impact, and he resolved more than once to break with Bosie. On 8th November 1893, he wrote to Lady Queensberry – long divorced from her husband – to tell her that her son was 'sleepless, nervous, and rather hysterical'. More to the point, 'he does absolutely nothing, and is quite astray in life, and may... come to grief of some kind. His life seems to me aimless, unhappy and absurd.' The words suggest a threat of self-harm. Bosie was, Oscar continued, 'terribly young in temperament'. He suggested that the boy leave England for some months – to as far away as Egypt. Wilde reassured her of his friendship with Bosie, but the entreaty was self-serving too.

Lady Queensberry made the arrangements, but in angry correspondence insisted to Bosie that he break with Oscar for good. She was convinced 'he has the part of a Lord Henry Wootton to you'. Wilde would be 'the murderer of [Bosie's] soul' if so. From Egypt, Bosie defended Wilde. Though amused by the friends who joined him there – Reggie Turner, 'the boy-snatcher of Clement's Inn', as Oscar called him; E.F. Benson; Robert Hichens, fishing for material for his forthcoming novel, *The Green Carnation* – Douglas was frustrated, since Oscar refused to reply to his many imploring letters. He resorted to desperate measures, imploring Constance to intercede. She did, but the response of March 1894 was not encouraging. Oscar merely wrote by telegram, 'Time heals every wound but for many months to come I will neither write to you nor see you.'

Wilde was writing too well to be disturbed. In early 1894 he finished *An Ideal Husband*, a play which 'contains a great deal of the real Oscar', he felt. He had soon also written most of two other plays, 'A Florentine Tragedy' and 'La Sainte Courtesane' – both historical dramas, the first in blank verse. (Neither would be completed.) By August, he was working up an outline for what would be his last, greatest comedy, *The Importance of Being Earnest*. The title was an in-joke, referring to an obscure volume of boy-loving verse by John Gambril Nicholson, *Love in Earnest* (1892). The poet's love for a boy of this name pulsates through-out the book: ''Tis Ernest sets my heart a-flame.'

Douglas acted intrepidly, returning from Egypt to Paris in six days. He was sending telegrams constantly. When he arrived in Paris, hoping Oscar would be there, he found only a letter. Bosie sent a huge, desperate telegram, declaring that he did not know what he would do if Wilde did not come. With a history of suicides in the Queensberry family, Oscar knew his duty. He duly turned up.

The pair arrived back in London on 31st March 1894. Bosie's appalling relationship with his father had encouraged the latter to watch his relationship with Oscar closely. The Marquess of Queensberry may have founded the rules of modern boxing, but as an opponent he rarely played fairly. He thought his son's failure to take his degree in Oxford a scandalous waste of time and effort. He seems to have intrinsically understood Bosie's sexual tastes. For both these matters, he blamed Wilde's supposed influence in what he called a 'most loathsome and dis-gusting relationship.' Queensberry immediately began hound-ing them intemperately. He threatened to disinherit Bosie, a serious matter for the unemployed idler, who, like his father, was incapable of a calm response. Douglas replied: 'WHAT A FUNNY LITTLE MAN YOU ARE.' Wilde would later call it 'a telegram of which the commonest street-boy would have been ashamed'. As a father, he had decided views about how sons should address their fathers.

After a sojourn in Florence, where they arrived – discreetly – separately, the pair returned. This time, Queensberry pursued Oscar to Tite Street. *De Profundis* recorded Wilde's impressions of the unannounced visit of 30th June, 'in my library... waving his small hands in the air in epileptic fury, your father, with his bully, or his friend, between us, had stood, uttering every foul word his foul mind could think of, and screaming the loathsome threats he afterwards with such cunning carried out'. Some intimate correspondence had reached Queensberry, occasioning especial anger. Douglas emboldened Wilde, and wrote non-chalantly to his father, 'I write to inform you that I treat your absurd threats with absolute indifference.' He himself took to carrying a pistol, which he even fired in a restaurant by mistake. In *De Profundis*, Oscar alleged that Bosie had used him in a never-ending struggle between father and son, 'The prospect of a battle in which you would be safe delighted you.'

Wilde now consulted lawyers, only to find that his preference, George Lewis, had been signed up by Queensberry for any imminent legal action. Between August and October, Oscar went on holiday with his family to Worthing, taking the unfinished manuscript of *The Importance of Being Earnest*. At one point, Bosie invited himself along, acknowledging later to Ross that 'the strain of being a bone of contention between Oscar and Mrs Oscar began to make itself felt' there. Bosie felt caught between the couple, as Oscar did between his beloved and his father.

In September 1894, Robert Hichens published *The Green Carnation* anonymously. Its 'Lord Reggie and Mr Amarinth' stood in lamely for Wilde and Douglas. Though the fiction was not strong, some details were sharply observed and the timing of the satire could not have been worse. Wilde initially claimed delight, congratulating the author by telegraph. He became more worried, though, as rumours circulated that he was its author. By October he was obliged to write to the *Pall Mall*

Gazette to deny the accusations, 'I invented that magnificent flower. But with the middle-class and mediocre book that usurps its strangely beautiful name I have, I need hardly say, nothing whatsoever to do. The flower is a work of art. The book is not.'

Wilde spent his fortieth birthday alone in Brighton. Bosie was at the Grand Hotel nearby, where they had first fled after Worthing disagreed with him. They saved money by moving into lodgings, but after nursing Douglas through a bad cold, Wilde found himself unattended when he fell ill himself. Instead, Bosie raged at Oscar's perceived indolence, returning to the Grand alone. Wilde was too weak to leave bed, and even went without water. Douglas wrote triumphantly on Oscar's birthday from the Grand, indicating that he was charging all expenses to Wilde. He also wrote two lines of such shallowness that Oscar never forgave them. The first was, 'When you are not on your pedestal you are not interesting.' The second was, 'The next time you are ill I will go away at once.'

It has long been suspected that Queensberry's first son, Francis, Viscount Drumlanrig, did not die accidentally in October 1894, but killed himself, fearing exposure as the lover of Lord Rosebery, then Foreign Secretary. The likelihood of this will never be known – our only sources are suspect. To Queensberry, in any case, after losing one son, the prospect of keeping Bosie pure – or away from Wilde, at least – became an obsession. Wilde was initially prepared to tell Queensberry he would never see Bosie again when he read in the paper of Drumlanrig's death. As ever, he weakened, telegraphing his condolences to Bosie instead.

In December 1894, Wilde gave a short set of epigrams, 'Phrases and Philosophies for the Use of the Young', to a young Oxford undergraduate, Jack Bloxam. Bloxam was to reprint them in a magazine of only one edition, *The Chameleon*. It would never have mattered, except that Bloxam included his own boldly homoerotic tale, 'The Priest and the Acolyte'. Wilde did not particularly like it. Still, it was 'at moments poisonous: which is something'. It was indeed to be something poisonous to Wilde.

The magazine did not give the name of the author of the story, leading many, including Queensberry, to think it was Wilde's work.

An Ideal Husband was rehearsed that month, opening on 5th January 1895 to great reviews. By the 17th, Wilde and Bosie had left for Algeria, a place much visited by western men seeking boys. Constance, ignorant of her husband's whereabouts, had to ask Ross for his address; she needed money to cover a month's stay in Torquay for herself and the boys. André Gide, meanwhile, happened to be in Blidah when the pair arrived. He checked out of the hotel when he saw their names, but reconsidered. All three dined together; the next day, they returned to Algiers. After a furious row, Douglas took a local boy to Biskra, leaving Wilde and Gide in the city. This is where, according to Gide's memoir *Si le grain ne meurt* (1926; published as *If It Die* in English), Wilde suggested he had fallen for a local flute-player. Gide confirmed it, and Wilde made the necessary arrangements with the boy. The two writers spent several days together, Wilde confiding in Gide about Queensberry's harrying. Gide was concerned about Wilde's proposed return, asking, 'Do you realise the risk?' Wilde replied, 'My friends advise me to be prudent. Prudent! How could I be that? It would mean going backward. I must go as far as possible.'

Wilde returned via Paris for his next opening. Bosie tactfully stayed in Algeria. *The Importance of Being Earnest* was to open on 14th February 1895. That day the police were called after Queensberry promised to interrupt the performance. Wilde advised producer George Alexander to cancel Queensberry's ticket. When he could not penetrate the theatre, the Marquess left Wilde a vegetable bouquet. Still, the critics agreed on the brilliance of *Earnest*, set to be another huge hit. *The New York Times* confidently announced, 'Oscar Wilde may be said to have at last, and by a single stroke, put his enemies under his feet.'

On 28th February 1895, Wilde was advised by his solicitor, Charles Humphreys, not to prosecute Queensberry for his conduct. The refusal of theatre staff to testify in respect of his behaviour was critical. Meanwhile, Bosie returned, joining Wilde at his rooms in the Avondale Hotel, Piccadilly. He immediately proposed inviting a boy to stay there with him at Oscar's expense. When Wilde objected, Douglas left for another hotel, accusing him by letter of weakness. An hour later, this and his father's next provocation would prove decisive in motivating Oscar to act. Wilde called in at the Albemarle Club, where a porter gave him Queensberry's card, left for him over a week earlier. On it was scrawled: 'To Oscar Wilde, posing somdomite' (for 'sodomite').

Wilde would later tell More Adey that, on receiving the two pieces of venom from father and son, 'I felt I stood between Caliban and Sporus.' To Ross, he wrote, 'My whole life seems ruined by this man… On the sand is my life spilt.' Ross cautioned Oscar against retaliation, and may have persuaded him to leave for Paris. But Wilde could not go. His luggage had been seized by the Avondale until he could settle the bill. Douglas urged Oscar to act unafraid. 'It is what we fear that happens to us,' he predicted rashly. Even without funds, Wilde should proceed. Bosie told him his brother Percy and his mother would pay legal costs – to satisfy themselves in punishing Queensberry. On 1st March, the playwright went to Marlborough Street police station to ask for a warrant for Queensberry's arrest on grounds of libel.

The case was initially adjourned. On 7th March, Wilde, Douglas and Constance attended *Earnest* together. On the 9th, George Lewis, Wilde's old friend, announced he could act no further in Queensberry's defence. He was replaced by Edward Carson, from Trinity College, Dublin. Wilde commented acidly, 'No doubt he will perform his task with the added bitterness of an old friend.' By the 12th, an ebullient Bosie had reassured Oscar of his imminent triumph so comprehensively that they set off to Monte Carlo for a week's recuperation.

Trials

At the Old Bailey on 3rd April, Wilde was hugely outflanked. Queensberry had been digging for more evidence. His solicitor, Charles Russell, worked with a private detective, Littlechild, who had learnt where Alfred Taylor lodged – a flat at 13 Little College Street. He broke in to find a post-box listing all the boys working from the premises. Littlechild took notes, pursued each, and threatened them unless they agreed to testify. Queensberry's defence thus named ten of twelve boys whom, they argued, Wilde had paid to commit sodomy on fifteen separate occasions. It also argued that Wilde's own writings were corrupting.

Humphreys had prepared Wilde for the latter possibility at least. He secured Frank Harris' agreement to testify that *Dorian Gray* was not immoral. But Harris, learning of the letters and other evidence, told Wilde bluntly to abandon the case, 'You haven't a dog's chance, and the English despise the beaten… Don't commit suicide.' Over lunch at the Café Royal with Wilde and Shaw, Harris outlined a plan whereby Wilde could pull out, taking his family to Paris until all subsided. Shaw approved. Then, according to Harris, Bosie appeared, screaming, 'Such advice shows you are no friend of Oscar's.' Wilde meekly followed Douglas out, repeating, 'No, it is not friendly.'

Edward Clarke, Wilde's counsel, opened. He was 'quiet and conversational' according to Harris, but Carson would soon be cross-examining Wilde much more forcefully and skilfully for

Queensberry's defence. Wilde testified well concerning the attempted blackmail over the letter. First Alfred Wood, then a man named Allen had approached Wilde for money. Allen argued that a 'very curious construction could be put upon that letter'. Oscar replied that as 'a work of art' alone it was valuable. He refused to give the £60 asked, handing Allen half a sovereign cab fare. A third man, Robert Clibborn, came to Tite Street offering Wilde the original letter for free. Allen had told him, 'there is no use trying to rent you [i.e. Wilde] as you only laugh at us'. There was hilarity in court at Wilde's response to the letter's poor condition, 'I think it quite unpardonable that better care was not taken of an original manuscript of mine,' he told Clibborn. There were other good moments. Wilde recounted Queensberry's visit to Tite Street, his allegation that he and Douglas had been 'kicked out of the Savoy Hotel at a moment's notice for [their] disgusting conduct'. This Wilde called 'a lie'. Queensberry had proposed thrashing Wilde if he was again seen with Bosie. Wilde had replied, 'I don't know what the Queensberry rules are, but the Oscar Wilde rule is to shoot at sight.'

We now know, however, that Clarke made a tactical error even mentioning the 'Hyacinthus' letter. He assumed Carson knew all about it – but he was wrong. Clarke thus donated his opponent a weight of additional evidence, however inconclusive, relating to Wilde's relations with boys and tendency to be blackmailed. The matter of Oscar's habitual deceit over his age provided an easy first score for Carson, too, in cross-examination. They had been college peers. Carson was forty-one. Wilde could not possibly be the thirty-nine he claimed. Oscar conceded the point.

Next, Carson turned to literature, starting with 'The Priest and the Acolyte's' deathbed 'kiss of perfect love'. Wilde thought the scene was 'disgusting twaddle'. Carson then raked through Wilde's own publications. On *Dorian Gray*, Wilde stuck to the simplest, aesthetic doctrine: that corruption was in the eye of the beholder – namely reader – and that 'the views of the Philistine on art could not be counted; they are incalculably stupid.' Carson had already insisted that Wilde had 'left it open to be inferred… that the sins of Dorian Gray, some of them, may have been sodomy.' Oscar argued that the reader determined the matter, since 'he who has found the sin has brought it.'

He was often funny, but the implicit superiority in Wilde's position, while amusing, was damaging too:

Carson: The affection and the love that is pictured of the artist towards Dorian Gray… might lead an ordinary individual to believe it had a sodomitical tendency, might it not?
Wilde: I have no knowledge of the ordinary individual.

Asked about his feelings for other men, Wilde preferred to admit plagiarism. In respect of Basil's 'ador[ation]' of Dorian, he said 'it was borrowed… from Shakespeare's sonnets.' Carson began throwing his favourite adjective around the courtroom. Sometimes, he must have thought, it would stick:

Carson: I believe you have written an article pointing out that Shakespeare's sonnets were practically sodomitical.
Wilde: On the contrary, Mr Carson, I wrote an article to prove that they were not so.

He raised the matter of the corrupting book in *Dorian Gray*, forcing Wilde to identify this as *À Rebours*, then to deny having done so. Again, Carson glossed Huysmans's novel as 'a book dealing with undisguised sodomy… a sodomitical book'.

Clarke, acknowledging the seriousness of Carson's assaults, parried the next day by quoting extensively from Queensberry's letters to Bosie. They showed how crazed Queensberry had become. Again, the strategy was misconceived. The underlying message for the jury was that, however extreme, Queensberry's volatility was driven by a paternal regard for Bosie's character.

As Carson put it, his client had 'one hope alone – that of saving his son'.

Carson handled with innuendo details concerning Wilde's chosen associates – their odd professions, for example, a valet, a groom, 'a newspaper boy out of employment' whom Wilde had given a cane. Wilde joked, 'I recognize no social distinctions at all of any kind and to me youth – the mere fact of youth – is so wonderful that I would sooner talk to a young man half an hour than ever be, well, cross-examined in court.' His flippancy, once an asset, was now a liability, and the cause of a fatal slip. Carson raised the name of Walter Grainger, a servant boy in Oxford named as having committed sodomy with Wilde repeatedly, both in Douglas' rooms and in Goring:

> Carson: Did you ever kiss him?
> Wilde: Oh, no, never in my life; he was a peculiarly plain boy... I thought him unfortunately – his appearance was so very unfortunately – very ugly – I mean – I pitied him for it...
> Carson: Do you say that in support of your statement that you never kissed him?
> Wilde: No, I don't; it is like asking me if I kissed a doorpost; it is childish.

Oscar was suddenly defensive, muttering that Carson was 'try[ing] to unnerve me in every way'. He conceded his mistake here, too – that of implying that any boy might be kissed: 'At times one says things flippantly when one should speak more seriously.'

Carson's closing speech cleverly discounted the possibility that Wilde was guilty of misconduct towards Bosie. However, he announced his intention to introduce a number of boys who could testify to the 'shocking acts' Wilde had initiated. This would be devastating. Suddenly, on day three, with Wilde absent from court, Clarke offered to abandon the case, albeit by way of complex manipulation of Queensberry's original Plea of Justification. But Carson insisted that the entire original plea stand. The judge, Mr Justice Collins, agreed, and compelled an acquittal from the jury. Queensberry was not guilty of libelling Wilde. Collins also wrote directly to Carson in praise: 'I never heard a more powerful speech nor a more searching crossXam.'

Queensberry's card had ambiguously argued that Wilde was either 'posing' as a sodomite, or was a posing sodomite. However, the fact that this was not libellous left Wilde highly vulnerable to arrest for sodomy. Meanwhile, Bosie's father may indirectly have told Oscar, 'I will not prevent your flight, but if you take my son with you, I will shoot you like a dog.' Wilde consulted rapidly with Humphreys, and then met Bosie, his brother Percy and Ross in the Holborn Viaduct Hotel. He wrote a quick letter of self-justification to the *Evening News* pointing out that in order to prove his case he would have required Bosie to testify, 'Rather than put him in so painful a position I determined to retire from the case, and to bear on my own shoulders whatever ignominy and shame might result.' Characteristically, Wilde was drawn to the role of martyr.

At five o'clock sharp, a summons was issued. Wilde was to be arrested on charges of 'committing acts of gross indecency'. Hiding in the Cadogan Hotel, Chelsea, with Ross and Reggie Turner, he was urged to take the boat train for France immediately. Constance was consulted and likewise urged flight. Wilde, however, had a resilience or fatalism amounting to folly. Like his mother in her own conflicts, he determined to stand his ground, 'I shall stay and do my sentence, whatever it is.' At 6.10 p.m., two detectives arrived, and took a semi-drunk Wilde to Bow Street station. Ross immediately went to Tite Street to pack a change of clothes. He realised too that there could be more – and worse – incriminatory evidence among Oscar's papers. He and a servant broke into the library. Ross carried a stack of correspondence away.

Ross was himself shamed by long public association with Wilde, and soon left for France. He was not alone. With poetic licence, one acquaintance noted that six hundred gentlemen had crossed to Calais that evening, not the usual sixty. Douglas did not flee, confident – for once correctly – of immunity from prosecution. Wilde sought bail, but it could not be arranged, primarily as only one figure approached – Bosie's brother – would now stand surety. Wilde's name was removed from the boards of both theatres; *Husband* and *Earnest* were soon taken off. Some of Oscar's friends, in Britain and in France, peeled away, denying any acquaintance. A rump remained loyal. A few – not all – of the boys named as Wilde's fellow sodomites would testify against him in court. Bosie got to at least one, Sidney Mavor, reminding him of his public school background and duty. Mavor subsequently testified that nothing had happened in bed with Oscar. Others were understandably tempted by money, accommodation and a promise of immunity from prosecution. Alfred Taylor would not betray his friend, so was then charged alongside him. The association further blighted Wilde's prospects.

Hearings began on 6th April. Wilde was kept in a cell in Bow Street, then in Holloway Prison. He remained largely silent. Oscar had cause to be in low spirits. By 24th April, Queensberry had forced a bankruptcy sale of his belongings, helped by many angry creditors. Though earning well, Wilde had no financial acumen, and had lived beyond his means for years. It is estimated that he was £6000 in debt. Bailiffs occupied Tite Street. Wilde's book collection, Newdigate Prize bust and furnishings were sold off for next-to-nothing. Queensberry wrote to one newspaper denying that he was capable of any 'sympathy' for Wilde, raving, 'I have helped to cut up and destroy sharks. I had no sympathy for them, but may have felt sorry, and wished to put them out of pain as far as possible.'

Bosie was making matters infinitely worse with his own interventions. He wrote hot-headed letters to the press – 'simply to say that you hated your father', as *De Profundis* has it. Still, at least he visited the prisoner daily. Wilde wrote to Ada Leverson that, though lonely, he was consoled by this 'slim thing, goldhaired like an angel, stand[ing] always at my side'. Clarke, however, felt Douglas' presence – in the country, even, let alone in court – would be prejudicial, and insisted he go to Paris.

The trial ran from 26th to 29th April. It was extraordinarily explicit in its allusions to sexual acts. The diversity among its participants was singular. Beerbohm recalled having to walk past 'a knot of renters... who were allowed to hang around after giving their evidence, and to wink at likely persons'. Various Savoy Hotel employees testified that they had seen boys in Wilde's bed, possibly confusing his room with Bosie's. One mentioned 'dirt'-stained bed-sheets. Wilde was forced under cross-examination to deny that anything said by these staff was true.

All the previous incidents and players were reintroduced, supplemented by the unstable Edward Shelley, who testified for the prosecution. Charles Gill, another Anglo-Irish Protestant, acted for the Crown, not Carson. Wilde's performance, if uneven, had moments of striking pathos, though he appeared 'careworn and anxious' (*The New York Times*). He was again represented by Clarke, who would not take a fee – recognition that he had served his client inadequately the first time. It augured badly, but Wilde was broke. He had no choice but to accept.

Gill introduced the magazine *The Chameleon*, in particular Douglas' phrase 'the love that dare not speak its name'. The defendant was asked to gloss this 'love'. For once, Wilde rallied. He became his old confident, articulate self – 'perfectly self-possessed,' noted Beerbohm. Oscar was most ardent, perhaps, in defending Bosie's words and honour, not his own:

The 'Love that dare not speak its name' in this century is such a great affection of an elder for a younger man as there was between David and Jonathan, such as Plato made the very basis of his philosophy, and such as you find in the sonnets of Michelangelo and Shakespeare. It is that deep spiritual affection that is as pure as it is perfect. It dictates and pervades great works of art like those of Shakespeare and Michelangelo, and those two letters of mine, such as they are. It is in this century misunderstood, so much misunderstood that it may be described as the 'Love that dare not speak its name,' and on account of it I am placed where I am now. It is beautiful, it is fine, it is the noblest form of affection. There is nothing unnatural about it. It is intellectual, and it repeatedly exists between an elder and a younger man, when the elder has intellect, and the younger man has all the joy, hope and glamour of life before him.

Wilde was applauded hard from the gallery. In Beerbohm's recollection, he 'carried the whole court right away'. He shrewdly did not emphasise here the necessity of the boy's beauty. The speech was actually an amalgam of two sections from *Dorian Gray*, but Wilde might be forgiven for resorting to self-plagiarism. The sentiment was what Oscar believed. As he wrote to Bosie on the 29th, resigned to being jailed but already holding out hopes of a future reconciliation abroad, 'Our love was always beautiful and noble, and if I have been the butt of a terrible tragedy, it is because the nature of that love has not been understood.'

Clarke was more impressive too, pointing out the various contradictions among the boys' statements and testimonies. Gill brought the jury's attention back to the 'unholy passion' n Wilde's letters to Douglas. Mr Justice Charles summed up, however, rather favourably. He discounted the literary allegations and disputed the hotel staff's stories, expressly mentioning that stained sheets may have an innocent cause.

The jury could not reach a verdict. Wilde faced near-immediate retrial. Meanwhile, though stiff conditions were applied, he secured bail with funds from Percy Douglas and one Rev. Stuart Headlam, who scarcely knew him. On 7th May,

Wilde was freed. He made for the Midland Hotel, St Pancras, where the manager told him he was unwelcome. This happened at another hotel. Wilde was obliged to head for 146 Oakley Street, where Willie lived with his new wife, and with Lady Wilde, their mother. 'Willie,' his abject brother begged, 'give me shelter or I shall die in the streets.' Willie took the opportunity to lord it over his disgraced brother. Lady Speranza, meanwhile, endlessly insisted that Oscar must stay and be tried. Others again urged Wilde to flee – even Percy Douglas, who stood to lose a fortune if the bail money were forfeit. Frank Harris came up with a yacht.

Wilde would not go. He did, however, accept the Leversons' offer of house-room, arriving around the 18th. In the many conversations with Ada which she later wrote up, Oscar made the famous quip about Dickens, 'One must have a heart of stone to read the death of Little Nell without laughing.' He was seeking humour in the tragedy of his own situation too. Other friends rallied. Yeats produced a set of letters from Irish writers offering courage to their compatriot. Constance visited her husband, begging him to flee. Instead, he filled his time writing passionately to Bosie. For his part, Douglas replied fondly, but his indiscreet lobbying for Wilde in France was not helpful. He told one journalist there were more than a hundred known homosexuals in the best English society. He even wrote to Henry Labouchere, enclosing a pamphlet urging reform of his own law against homosexual acts.

The next trial began on 22nd May at the Old Bailey. Queensberry attended. He had begun writing abusive notes to his former wife and his son Percy, with whom he was involved in a street brawl the previous evening. Alfred Taylor was now tried separately and found guilty – though only of 'indecency', not sodomy. Still, this cast a shadow over Wilde's prospects. Clarke repeatedly insisted on the unreliability of the blackmailing witnesses, and of Shelley, who insisted Wilde had abused and degraded him. Sir Frank Lockwood, the Solicitor-General, concluded for the prosecution with what Wilde later called 'an appalling denunciation' of his character, 'like a thing out of Tacitus, like a passage in Dante'. Mr Justice Wills's summoning up was distinctly unfavourable. On 25th May, after a couple of hours' discussion, the jury returned to find Wilde guilty.

Wills immediately addressed both Wilde and Taylor in grave terms. 'People who can do these things,' he insisted, 'must be dead to all sense of shame.' Both must be given the maximum possible sentence – two years' imprisonment with hard labour. Someone in court shouted: 'Shame!' But Yeats wrote that the women prostitutes outside danced with joy. 'The High Priest of the Decadents', as one gloating editorial put it, had been destroyed. Wilde is said to have asked before being taken down, 'And I? May I say nothing, my lord?'

Prison, Demise and Last Writings: England and Abroad 1895–1900

Wilde will always be seen as a martyr by some. His career, in his lifetime, was destroyed in the English courts. Arguably the hard labour and demoralisation together destroyed both his spirits and bodily health. Yeats argued that 'the Britisher's jealousy of art and the artist' lay behind his prosecution. Others have argued that the Liberal Party needed a high-profile victim under the gross indecency statute to distract the press from rumours attending Lord Rosebery. Oscar hardly discouraged the idea that he was a martyr. By adopting the name 'Sebastian' on his release, he identified himself with the Roman saint who had had to be martyred twice before dying. Sebastian, too, was the religious figure that had most readily allowed artists to indulge any interest in the sensuality of the male form. Guido Reni's portrait of Sebastian, which Oscar saw in Genoa as a student, was among his favourite paintings.

He was first taken to Pentonville Prison. The wooden bed had sheets and rugs but no mattress. A tin pot was provided for his toilet, but it could only be emptied three times daily. Breakfast was cocoa and bread. Chapel followed. Dinner at twelve alternated between bacon with beans, cold meat, suet pudding and soup. An evening meal at five thirty might be porridge with bread. Prison clothes were coarse, dull and marked with arrows. Wilde was compelled to walk a treadmill senselessly for six hours each day, and allowed to exercise outdoors for one hour. He was also forced to make postbags or sew. For three months he had no outside contact; then he was allowed to write one letter and to receive just one. Three visitors would also be granted twenty minutes. After another three months, the same privileges would be given. The regime was brutal, as Wilde would later argue, involving three 'permanent punishments authorized by law' – hunger, insomnia and illness. The first he suffered constantly; the second, nightly, as he shivered with cold; the third repeatedly, partly through malnutrition. Portions were standardised; Wilde's size meant he suffered more. He lost much weight.

Reading matter was officially denied. Wilde had been given the Bible and Bunyan's *Pilgrim's Progress*, however. He told the prison inspector Haldane that he longed for Flaubert. Haldane thought there was scope for clemency, but an author like Flaubert would not be permitted. Wilde instead asked for fifteen books. All were non-contentious – Augustine, Pascal, Newman – except the last: Pater's *Renaissance*. The Secretary of State gave special approval. On 4th July, Wilde was moved to Wandsworth Prison. Meanwhile, Constance, who had fled to Switzerland with Cyril and Vyvyan, was considering divorce. Reassured, however, by her brother Otho's petitioning of Wilde by letter, that what he wanted above all was for the family to stay together, she relented. On 9th September, she wrote to the prison governor asking if she might visit her husband.

Bosie had asked for permission to write in August, but as only one correspondent was permitted – namely, Constance – the request was refused. Robert Sherard brought news on 26th August that Douglas was planning to publish an account of his relationship with Wilde in France, even including several uncompromising love letters. This, Wilde saw, risked jeopardising everything he might now hope for: reconciliation with his wife and children, a lessening of his sentence, or reconsideration of the prison conditions. Unable to write directly, he begged Sherard to get Bosie to stop.

Douglas meant well, but his judgment was seriously awry. At Le Havre, he hired a yacht and cabin boy. They, and friends, caused a scandal by bathing naked. Douglas wrote indignantly to the 'little provincial newspaper' that was stirring things up that he could handle their machinations, 'but it is different for my little cabin boy, an innocent creature'. In the French press, several supportive pieces on Wilde had appeared, but Douglas could not appreciate the difference between these stoic assessments and his own franker celebration of their relationship:

I shall not pretend that the friendship between Mr Wilde and myself was an ordinary friendship nor simply an intellectual friendship, nor even that it was like the feeling which an older brother might have for his younger. No, I say now frankly... that our friendship was love, real love – love, it is true, completely pure but extremely passionate. Its origin was, in Mr Wilde, a purely physical admiration for beauty and grace (*my* beauty and *my* grace); it matters little whether they are real... what must be remarked is that it was a perfect love, more spiritual than sensual, a truly Platonic love, the love of an artist for a beautiful mind and a beautiful body.

In terms of Wilde's relations with Constance, these were clearly the words of an envious suitor, and could not have been more provocative. Douglas only withdrew the article in the light of Wilde's clear instructions. He kept an open mind on whether he might publish it in future.

In late September 1895, Wilde was declared bankrupt. Days earlier, he had been allowed a visit from Constance, who found the experience 'awful, more so than I had any conception it could be'. The extent of Wilde's rejection of his recent conduct seemed clear, 'he has been mad the last three years', his wife reported Oscar as saying. She decided to stand by her 'weak rather than wicked' spouse, though she adopted a fictitious surname,

'Holland'. Douglas, meanwhile, grew frustrated, hearing third-hand of Oscar's changed view of himself. His ill-judged reaction in a letter to More Adey of 30th November indicates how enduringly adolescent Bosie remained, 'I am not in prison but I think I suffer as much as Oscar and in fact more… Tell him I know that I have ruined his life, that everything is my fault, if that pleases him. I don't care.'

October saw Wilde down with dysentery. His illness inspired petitions for him to be freed. But many friends, well-wishers and associates such as Henry James and Emile Zola would not sign such a document. On 21st November, after fainting in chapel, Wilde was moved to Reading Prison. An injury to the right ear that resulted from the fall would plague him ever after. At Clapham Junction station, in handcuffs, he was spat on and ridiculed by the crowds.

At Reading, still weak, he was given menial duties, overseeing the library. February 1896, meanwhile, saw the first production of *Salome* in Paris. It was well-received, and attended by Beardsley, at least. There was sadder news. On the 19th, Constance arrived from Genoa, to tell Wilde that his mother had died on 3rd. Jane had asked for Oscar to be allowed to visit in her last days, but this was refused. She asked that nobody attend her own funeral. Wilde was heartened by Constance's thoughtful, gentle character at this meeting; she found Oscar 'an absolute wreck compared with what he was'.

In his second year at Reading, Wilde was given a greater range of books, including Chaucer, and Pater's latest work. May 1896 saw Ross's first visit. He had heard that Douglas planned a publication of his own verse, dedicated to Wilde. Wilde curtly wrote the next day, 'I could not accept or allow such a dedication. The proposal is revolting and grotesque.' Wilde referred to his lover as 'Douglas' throughout, asking Ross to demand on his behalf the return of all letters, jewellery and other possessions. He encouraged Ross to quote from the letter directly, so that Douglas might know he was asking on Wilde's instruction.

Douglas was astonished. He withdrew the volume for the moment – it appeared later that year, without a dedication – but did not return the letters. They alone stood between him and suicide. Even so, '[i]f Oscar asks me to kill myself, I will do so, and he shall have back the letters when I am dead.' Though honouring Wilde's earlier request not to publish, Douglas had gone ahead with a new version of his article on Wilde, which appeared in *La Revue blanche* on 1st June. He spelt out exactly what he and Wilde were, and why he thought such people worth defending, 'Oscar Wilde is now suffering for being a uranian [a preferred literary term for male homosexual], a Greek, a sexual man.' That same month, ironically, Wilde was appealing for early release from jail, citing precisely the sexual 'madness' Douglas sought to celebrate. Wilde even invoked the vicious slander of his character in Max Nordau's *Degeneration* (first published in English in 1895) to spell out how ill he had been, and still was. (After his release, Wilde was happy to defend 'Uranian' affections in private letters. To Ross, he wrote, 'To have altered my life would have been to have admitted that Uranian love is ignoble. I hold it to be noble – more noble than other forms.')

June also saw a visit from Frank Harris, part of the ongoing attempts to have Wilde released. Harris found his friend older and thinner, and asked what he considered unjust about his treatment. 'The list of my grievances would be without end,' replied Wilde. He was forever being punished for small or imaginary misdemeanours, and being accused of malingering when genuinely ill. Wilde feared above all the insanity to which he felt prison was systematically pushing him. Colonel Isaacson, the Reading governor, responded to any enquiry by insisting on Wilde's good health, confirmed by the prison doctors whom Wilde despised.

Douglas, meanwhile, ignored the petitions to return Wilde's things. On 20th September, he told Adey, 'I have determined to regard anything he says now as non-existent. If he continues in the same strain after leaving it will be another matter.' He added bitterly, 'Of my undying (I use the word in its real sense not that in which he so often used it to me) love and devotion to him he may rest assured whether he continues to deserve it or not.' It is easy to object to Bosie's petulance. But self-interested as these letters may be, they are also the outpourings of a passionate lover, suddenly jilted. Douglas' assumption – that prison had somehow got to Wilde, who would become his usual (dissolute) self on release – would prove a shrewder assessment of his lover's character than everyone else's hopes.

On reflection, too, Wilde told Ross in November that he could not judge Bosie for much, as he had 'passions merely', not 'unworthy motives'. Such a character could not be held accountable for his conduct, 'Do not think that I would blame *him* for my vices. He had as little to do with them as I had with his. Nature was in this matter a stepmother to each of us.' In one specific, however, Wilde did find Bosie culpable, 'I blame him for not appreciating the man he ruined.' Within months, in *De Profundis*, Oscar would come up with a still more baroque formulation, emphasising his own impressionable character, not Bosie's, 'But most of all I blame myself for the entire ethical degradation I allowed you to bring onto me. The basis of character is will-power, and my will-power became absolutely subject to yours.' The toughening of Wilde's views, as most fully expressed in *De Profundis*, stemmed not from what Douglas had said or done, but from the fact that he had not contacted Wilde. Letters were now freely allowed, yet Douglas wrote only to mediators such as Ross, whom he blamed for turning Oscar against him. Bosie was petulant and unforgiving in respect of Constance's early assumption of her place as first-entitled visitor. He was furious too that Ross had been able to cross the Channel to visit Wilde in prison.

Colonel Isaacson was replaced in July 1896 by Major Nelson, a much more sympathetic figure – 'the most Christlike man I ever met', as Oscar later put it. He permitted Wilde to write freely, and encouraged a long list of requested books for the Home Office to consider. In January 1897, Wilde began a long letter of self-justification – addressed to Bosie and commonly known as *De Profundis*, though Wilde's own provisional title was 'In carcere et vinculis'. The curious genre – an extensive self-examination in the form of a private letter – was necessitated by circumstance. Everything Wilde wrote in prison was submitted at the end of the day, to be returned only on his departure. What he wrote, therefore, had to flow logically and easily from memory. Wilde was writing literature, but was not pretending to correspond with Bosie; *De Profundis* was also a true plea for reconciliation. With occasional bitterness, Wilde noted Bosie's relative good fortune, railed against his temperamental excesses, but reserved most punishment for himself.

After three months, it was finished. *De Profundis* would first be published by Ross in bowdlerised form after Wilde's death, without reference to Douglas. Still, it had been a cathartic exercise too, reigniting recognition in Wilde of his literary gifts. In it, he may have mourned what he had lost through 'weakness', but he was also defiant in claiming a literary legacy, 'I was a man who stood in symbolic relation to the art and culture of my age'; 'I summed up all systems in a phrase, and all existence in an epigram.' Wilde toyed with resuming his writing career, telling one warder half-seriously, 'I am no longer the Sirius of Comedy. I have sworn solemnly to dedicate my life to Tragedy. If I write any more books, it will be to form a library of lamentation.'

On 1st April, Wilde asked for permission to send the letter to Ross, so he could copy it and forward the original to Bosie. The Home Office refused to allow this. Relations with Constance, meanwhile, cooled. His wife was keen to ensure an alteration in Oscar's spendthrift habits. His half of her dowry had been auctioned by the Receiver. She had bid, but been outbid by Ross and Adey, whom she thereafter felt were treacherous. They wanted only to protect Oscar financially in case relations with Constance turned bad. Her original offer to her husband – that he be given an allowance of £200 per annum – was reduced to £150. Wilde agreed to the terms, which involved handing over custody of his sons. He signed on 17th May, just before his release. Oscar agreed not to visit his family without permission, and – critically – not be involved in 'any moral misconduct or notoriously consort with evil or disreputable companions'. Both parties knew who was meant.

On 19th May, at 6.15 a.m., Wilde was free. He had left Reading the night before, since his formal release would be from Pentonville. Two journalists turned up. To one, Oscar said that he 'coveted neither notoriety nor oblivion'. He was first met by Adey and Rev. Headlam, at whose house he changed clothes and drank coffee. The Leversons appeared, Ada finding Oscar 'markedly better, slighter and younger than… two years previously'. Wilde seemed in good spirits, though Ross recalled that the prison governor had once said, 'He looks well. But like all men unused to manual labour who receives a sentence of this kind, he will be dead within two years.'

Wilde took the Newhaven night-boat for Dieppe, where he was met by Ross and Turner. His friends had booked him into the Hotel Sandwich, procured a list of books he had requested and secured £800 through petitions. A letter from Bosie requested a meeting. Wilde wrote, assuring him of his love, but insisting on waiting a little. They corresponded warmly and often, Douglas' anger now turning to repeated declarations of love, loyalty and atonement. But Oscar was torn. He also wrote Constance a letter she described as 'full of penitence'. He asked to meet; she stalled. In fact, though she did not explain it, Constance was experiencing a painful spinal paralysis from a longstanding injury. Bosie, by comparison, seemed avid for Oscar's company. Wilde's Lord Darlington had spoken for his author, 'I can resist anything except temptation.'

Wilde wrote several letters to the British press regarding the awfulness of prison conditions. He also wrote a last, major work, *The Ballad of Reading Gaol*, between June and July 1897. It was on a contemporary tragedy – the execution of Charles Thomas Wooldridge, a trooper in the Royal Horse Guards who had been hung in Reading Prison on 7th July 1896. Wooldridge had killed his wife out of sexual jealousy. Wilde had seen the scaffold. In 1898, the long poem was published in Britain, but not under Wilde's own name. 'C.3.3.' was used, his cell number in prison. He meant for the verse to underline the need for reform in Britain's prison and justice systems. Ross showed the poem to Major Nelson of Reading Prison beforehand, who found it 'a terrible mixture of good, bad and indifferent'.

Dieppe was full of the English. Of many former acquaintances, few were prepared to meet Wilde, however. Jacques-Emile Blanche, Aubrey Beardsley and Walter Sickert, all resident, shunned him. He was also being followed by a private detective employed by Queensberry. In such circumstances, Oscar did not have the will to stay in Dieppe for long, or apart from Bosie either. Though Wilde needed the allowance from Constance, he needed company too. He may wrongly have thought the £800 hard to exhaust. In May, he moved just five miles to a sleepy village, Berneval. Wilde took to it, and briefly considered settling in the country. He planned a new play, 'Pharaoh', in the style of *Salome* and possibly for Lugné-Poe, who had staged the earlier work. 'Ahab and Jezebel' was another likely subject. He met, and developed a passion for Ernest Dowson the poet. Dowson persuaded him to try a woman prostitute, which was not a success, 'like chewing cold mutton'.

On 19th June, André Gide turned up. They talked amicably, Gide reminding Wilde that he had predicted his own downfall in Algiers. Oscar concurred, 'it wasn't possible to go any further, and it couldn't last.' He embraced Gide's account of him in the recent *Les Nourritures terrestres*, adding, 'But dear, promise me from now on never to write *I* any more. In art, don't you see, there is no first person.' Of Douglas, he commented that prison had divided them – not literally so much as philosophically. Wilde accepted his shame but Douglas refused to consider his own. Hence, 'we cannot follow the same path... His is that of Alcibiades, mine is now that of St Francis of Assisi.'

It was wishful thinking. That month, Wilde's resolve had already collapsed. He knew Bosie was awaiting an invitation in Paris, and sent one around 8th June. Meanwhile, he had written offering Lady Queensberry 'conditions' for a prospective meeting with her son. Both he and Bosie needed to ensure they did not lose their allowances. She refused to help. Still, the invitation – to meet on the 19th – had been made. It did not come to pass. Wilde's solicitor discovered it and resigned. Oscar told Bosie not to come, since it was likely that his father had also heard of the plan. Queensberry had promised to visit Dieppe with a pistol, were they to meet. Douglas was furious at the change in arrangements, and again blamed Adey and Ross. Wilde claimed the delay was also necessary for him to finish a play. In truth he was blocked.

A large correspondence passed between Oscar and Bosie throughout the summer. Constance, meanwhile, wrote rarely. She finally agreed to meet – but only once she had the boys sent away. Wilde felt snubbed and humiliated, and wrote suggesting that her behaviour was forcing him back to Bosie. He missed his sons, and was deeply hurt. As he subsequently asked a journalist acquaintance, 'Is there any crime on earth so terrible that in punishment of it a father can be prevented from seeing his children?' Another invitation was sent to the 'boy' he could see, Bosie, on 20th August, suggesting they meet in neutral Rouen. Initially Douglas claimed he could not afford the fare, but thought better of it. By the 28th they were reconciled. Oscar burst into tears at the station. They talked, ate and stayed the night together. Douglas was obliged to meet his mother and sister imminently, but suggested they make secret plans to meet in Naples. While they were separated, Wilde effectively rescinded all he had expressed in *De Profundis*. Doubtless mindful of how blocked he had been in Dieppe, he wrote beautifully and romantically – if evidently also delusively – to Douglas:

I feel that my only hope of again doing beautiful work in art is being with you. It was not so in the old days, but now it is different... Everyone is furious with me for going back to you, but they don't understand us. I feel that it is only with you that I can do anything at all. Do remake my ruined life for me, and then our friendship and love will have a different meaning to the world.

Wilde knew his few friends would not understand. He could not help himself.

When they met in Aix-les-Bains for the journey to sexually relaxed Naples, neither had any money. Bosie asked his mother for another handout. Wilde, in desperation, approached composer Dalhousie Young for an advance on a libretto he had proposed. They scraped enough together to rent the Villa Guidice above the waterfront in Posillipo. It was smart but rat-infested. A witch was deployed for a suitable curse to expel the vermin. The pair wrote, but to little effect, Wilde 'improving' *The Ballad of Reading Gaol* for its imminent publication by the pornographer-publisher Leonard Smithers, whom he had met in France, and with whom Wilde had probably liaised in secret over the publication of *Teleny*. But Smithers preferred Wilde's original wording. They spent some days on Capri, which would inspire Jacques d'Adelswärd-Fersen's novel *Lord Lyllian* (1905), featuring Wilde and Douglas in fictional guise. Axel Munthe invited both to dinner at San Michele, the beautiful villa he had built in Anacapri. The ex-patriate community in Naples, meanwhile, kept them at arm's length.

Constance heard of her husband's recidivism. On 28th September, she wrote forbidding any return 'to your filthy, insane life'. There were lengthy discussions as to whether Oscar had broken the terms of their arrangement. He agreed that Bosie was 'a gilded pillar of infamy', but distinguished this from being disreputable. In November, nevertheless, Constance stopped Oscar's money, though she would occasionally relent, making one-off, anonymous donations through Ross. Wilde told Ross, 'Women are so petty, and Constance has no imagination.' What he did not know was that his supposed friends Adey and Ross had partially supported her actions. Likewise, Lady Queensberry sought to finish for good Bosie's indulgence in 'brandy, betting and boys'. She wrote threatening to cancel his allowance of about £350 per annum unless both signed a pledge that they would live apart. If they signed, she would grant Wilde a one-off payment of £200, and pay off any Naples debts Bosie had incurred. She knew her son.

The arrangement could not be passed up. They had been 'hunted out' (said Ross). In any case, as Bosie prevaricated throughout November 1897, it became clear that he was disillusioned with the post-prison Wilde. He felt a duty to help Oscar, but this was no longer tied to love. In his later writings, Douglas blamed Wilde for falling out of love with him because of his age, then twenty-seven. It is more likely that he tired of the eternal pariah status or poverty. Wilde's name had been ruined for ever by the trials. Douglas' had not. On 3rd December, Bosie left Naples for Rome, and did not return.

Wilde stayed on, as the villa was paid for until the end of January. The British consul mentioned his presence to Lord Rosebery, visiting his own villa nearby, but added that Wilde 'looks thoroughly abashed, much like a whipped hound... I really cannot think he will be any trouble to you, and after all, the poor devil must live somewhere.' On 13th February 1898, all but destitute, Wilde returned to Paris. That day, *Reading Gaol* saw publication in London. But Wilde's life was again in ruins. Douglas 'had offered me love, affection, and care, and promised that I should never want for anything', he wrote to Ross. On arriving in Naples, he had discovered that Douglas had no means, and again expected to live off Oscar's earnings. If this had ever been possible, it was now an absurd notion. Wilde described the experience as 'the most bitter... of a bitter life'. Nonetheless, his literary career was to experience one extraordinary last upturn. *The Ballad of Reading Gaol* by 'C.3.3.' sold in its thousands. People knew who the author was, though it was not till its seventh edition of June 1899 that Wilde's name was added to the title page.

He sent copies to Bosie, Ross, Adey, Charles Ricketts, the Leversons, Max Beerbohm, George Bernard Shaw, Ernest Dowson, Lionel Johnson, and to Reading's governor Major Nelson. Constance received an uninscribed copy of the poem, which she found 'frightfully tragic'. She had someone tell Oscar; he responded with a bold demand for the £78 he claimed she owed him. He also referred to Douglas. Constance told a friend, 'He says that he loved too much and that that is better than hate! This is true abstractly, but his was an unnatural love, a madness that I think is worse than hate.'

The poem was critically well-received. Arthur Symons called it 'a sombre, angry, interrupted reverie'. The *Pall Mall Gazette* saluted 'the most remarkable poem that has appeared this year'. Still, Wilde admitted to friends that he had now 'lost the joy of writing' – 'the intense energy of creation'. On a later occasion, Wilde was asked why he no longer wrote and answered, 'I wrote when I did not know life; now that I know the meaning of life, I have no more to write.' Smithers, meanwhile, published Wilde's two last plays, providing much-needed income.

Oscar's last two years – mostly in Paris – were pitiful. He drank, hired men and begged. Acquaintances were few. He met Gide a couple of times, but the old camaraderie was gone. Wilde too often demanded pity or cash. He earned some money from various literary commissions and permissions, some of which he did not fulfil and others of which he did not legitimately control. Still, even poverty Wilde contrived to make light of. To one acquaintance, he wrote, 'Like dear St Francis of Assisi, I am wedded to poverty, but in my case the marriage is not a success. I hate the bride that has been given to me.'

'Constance Holland' – as his wife was now known – died aged forty after an operation on her back on 7th April 1898. Aptly,

Bosie came to help Oscar grieve – though Ross, who also saw him, claimed Wilde 'did not feel it at all'. On her death, an instruction that he should not visit his sons was upheld, but an allowance of £150 per annum – little enough to Oscar, true – was restored without condition.

Douglas was also in Paris. They did not live together, but met frequently. Bosie was still a potential liability, gambling away much of his own allowance. Wilde commented, 'He has a faculty of spotting the loser which, considering that he knows nothing at all about horses, is perfectly astounding.' Douglas had also taken up with a stunning lover, Maurice Gilbert. Relations with his family were typically mutable. In November, Douglas returned to England to make peace with his father. He promised in a letter to his cousin that relations with Wilde were 'harmless'. They saw each other 'from time to time', but Bosie was motivated by pity for a 'poor and broken' friend. In any case, according to Wilde, Douglas was now 'devoted to a dreadful little ruffian aged fourteen'. Queensberry promised to restore Bosie's allowance when they met, but characteristically reneged afterwards until the situation with 'that beast Wilde' was clarified. Father and son fell out, predictably. Hostility was their default arrangement; reconciliation an occasional error.

In December 1898, a flush Frank Harris offered to take Wilde to the Côte d'Azur for three months. Oscar claimed to write better in a warm climate. It was a kind offer, installing his friend in a hotel near Cannes. Still, Harris himself had plenty to do, and when together, they seemed only to bicker – over the respective beauty of men and women, or rather, of boys and girls. In Nice, Wilde saw Sarah Bernhardt in *La Tosca*. She did not shun him. He took up with 'bare-limbed' 'fisher-lads' in the village where he was staying, La Napoule.

Wilde was next invited by a vague, closeted acquaintance, Harold Mellor, to Switzerland. He accepted all charity these days, and detoured so he could lay flowers on Constance's grave in Genoa. Wilde was heartbroken, however, to discover that his wife's tomb read 'Constance Mary, daughter of Harold Lloyd, Q.C.', as if he had never existed. He scarcely knew Mellor, who responded to his guest's heavy drinking by simply cutting down the quantity served. Wilde made his excuses and left for Paris.

On 13th March 1899, Willie Wilde died. The brothers were still estranged, and Oscar was not especially moved. He took to the cult of exile and increasingly shunned company, telling Max de Mores: 'I am a vagabond. The century will have had two vagabonds, Paul Verlaine and me.' Some who knew him failed to recognise the dishevelled figure. Others shunned him. One told Ross that Oscar 'was ruining what sympathy was left for him among the Parisians by showing himself drunk on the boulevards with Sodomist outcasts.'

In April 1900, Harold Mellor surprisingly asked Wilde to accompany him to Palermo, Rome and Switzerland. He did not loiter in the Eternal City, but Wilde did, staying on a month. On Easter Day, Oscar received the Pope's blessing, taking along one of the young boys from the streets. Then, back in Paris, a small miracle happened. A hotelier called Jean Dupoirier settled Wilde's debts at his previous lodgings and allowed him to stay at his own humble Hôtel d'Alsace, though Wilde was always in arrears. Oscar again met Bosie, who had come into a considerable inheritance on his father's death in January. But Wilde's suggestion of a small allowance struck Douglas as ridiculous. He retorted, 'I can't afford to spend anything except on myself.' Wilde was acting 'like an old fat prostitute'. Frank Harris helped by buying a plot from Oscar – 'Love is Law' – for £175. Harris worked it up into a successful play. *Mr and Mrs Daventry* opened in the autumn of Wilde's last year.

Wilde was suffering from ill-health, which he attributed to food poisoning from shellfish. His skin was irritable, frequently coming out in rashes. (There were other symptoms, which Ellmann traces to syphilis; others disagree.) By September 1900, Wilde was bedridden. On 10th October, he was operated upon for an ear infection. This was unsuccessful, and Oscar worsened.

Friends had time to travel from England. He had telegrammed Ross, 'Terribly weak. Please come.' There were several other visitors. To Lily Wilde, his sister-in-law, Oscar quipped something like: 'I am dying as I have lived – beyond my means.' They were not, as is often thought, his final words, but he also joked to Claire de Praz, 'My wallpaper and I are fighting a duel to the death. One or the other of us has to go.'

Wilde continued to drink much absinthe and champagne as his health deteriorated. He was ever deeper in debt, with no hope of settling the doctor's bills. An ear abscess developed, the inflammation spreading internally. Ross had to leave for a while to be with his mother on the Côte d'Azur. Reggie Turner stayed with Wilde through mid-November. On the 25th, a diagnosis of acute, inoperable cerebral meningitis was reached. From here on, Oscar drifted in and out of consciousness and even sanity. His temperature was so high that when Ross returned on the morning of 29th November, he left the hotel immediately to find a priest.

Father Cuthbert Dunne, a Dubliner resident in France, was found. He baptised Wilde and read the last rites. Oscar could not speak, but responded by raising his hand in assent. At half past five the following morning, 30th November 1900, a death rattle began. Ross reported that, minutes after his demise, Wilde's body exploded, fluid pouring out of several orifices. Oscar Wilde died as he had lived – inappropriately, outrageously, and with scant reference to what decorum demanded.

Afterlife

A requiem mass was said at St Germain-des-Prés, and Wilde was interred in Bagneux cemetery on 3rd December. There were fourteen mourners, including Bosie, who had arrived in town the day before. In the first carriage after the hearse were Douglas, Ross, Turner and the hotelier Dupoirier. When Wilde was lowered into his grave, Douglas was said to have been so overcome he almost fell in. A simple tombstone quoted from the Book of Job, 'After I spoke, they did not speak again, and my word dropped upon them.' Wilde would not rest there for ever. In 1909, Mrs Helen Carew commissioned the extravagant tomb carved by Jacob Epstein for his reburial in Père-Lachaise.

A year on, Douglas wrote a sweet if bland sonnet in tribute, 'To Oscar Wilde'. In 1905, Ross published the expurgated *De Profundis*. Bosie went unmentioned for legal reasons. But a 1912 biography of Wilde by Arthur Ransome led to Douglas suing the author for libel. In consequence, Ross was obliged to supply the whole of *De Profundis*, which was read out in court. Douglas continued to harry and denounce Ross, to the point where Ross in turn sued for libel, though unsuccessfully. He died in 1918, asking for his ashes to be placed in Wilde's tomb. This, clearly, would be too provocative to Douglas, and Ross's relatives held back. Finally, in November 1950, long after Douglas' death and on the fiftieth anniversary of Wilde's own, Ross joined his friend.

Meanwhile, Douglas had many years to rework his relationship with Wilde. In several accounts, he argued improbably that he had never committed homosexual acts. He would soften in later versions, but cannot be said to have ever offered full, reliable witness. He died in 1945, having written nothing substantial that did not relate to their relationship. Whether he liked it or not, Oscar and his legacy engulfed Douglas.

* * *

Wilde was famous early in life. He was enshrined in literature as early as 1877, at the age of twenty-three, after he met one Julia Constance Fletcher during his first stay in Rome. She rapidly penned a three-volume novel, *Mirage*, published under the pen-name 'George Fleming', and featuring a character, Claude Davenant, unmistakably based on Wilde. In 1880, an Oxford acquaintance, Rhoda Broughton, wrote another, based on Wilde's fame around the university, *Second Thoughts*. There was André Raffalovich's *A Willing Exile* (1890), featuring a fictional Oscar in 'Cyprian Broome'. Robert Hichens' satire on aestheticism, *The Green Carnation* (1894), clearly featured Wilde and Douglas. André Gide portrayed Wilde as the dissolute 'Ménalque' in his *Les Nourritures terrestres* (1897), translated as *Fruits of the Earth*. Nor did the tradition slow with Wilde's death. Baron Jacques d'Adelswärd-Fersen's eponymous hero *Lord Lyllian* (1905) is seduced on Capri by a Wildean character. Ronald Firbank wrote a novel that responded to *Salome*, *The Artificial Princess*. In his 1920 drama *The Princess Zoubaroff*, Firbank enshrined Wilde and Douglas as 'Lord Orkish' and 'Reggie Quintus'. Gradually there was a critical rehabilitation, and growing interest in Wilde's life story as the century progressed.

Capturing a life such as Wilde's today is especially hazardous. 'It is always Judas who writes the biography,' Oscar claimed. The tale is now somewhat familiar to many, yet its emphases have undergone extraordinary distortions across time and culture.

What Wilde was and what he did matters to an unusual volume of people. In recent memory, Neil Bartlett's *Who Was that Man?* interrogated Wilde as proto-martyr and gay icon. Alan Sinfield's *The Wilde Century* explained both how late twentieth-century 'gay politics' required Oscar to be these things, and how seismic shifts in how we conceive sexuality across the century mean this must be an illusion. Richard Ellmann's biography embraced his life's dominant narrative of tragic fall, emphasising Wilde's predisposition to doom and self-destruction. Neil McKenna, by contrast, stressed the implicit radicalism of Wilde's sexual politics and his ethical modernity. Terry Eagleton's play *Saint Oscar* emphasises Wilde's Irishness. Tom Stoppard's *The Invention of Love* casts him *in absentia* as sexual practitioner to Housman's theoretician. Neil Bartlett's *In Extremis* presents Wilde as superstitious. Moises Kaufman's *Gross Indecency* and David Hare's *The Judas Kiss* both depict him as scapegoat.

It is customary to emphasise that the writing is what endures, not the writer's life. Wilde's collected works do offer an extraordinarily rich 1500 pages, especially impressive over such a short period of composition. Yet it has fallen to him again to prove exceptional. For it is impossible to read these pages without reflecting on the circumstances of their author's life, and his demise in particular and the role they played in it. It is equally unimaginable that people in the near or distant future will ask: 'Who was Oscar Wilde?'

Chronological list of works

The fictional, dramatic, poetic and prose titles in the following table – with the exception of the disputed *Teleny* – are usefully collected in *The Complete Works of Oscar Wilde: Centenary Edition*, with introductions by Vyvyan Holland and Merlin Holland (London / Glasgow, 2000). However, *The Importance of Being Earnest* is only given there in its four-act version. A useful recent edition of the plays is *The Importance of Being Earnest and Other Plays: 'Lady Windermere's Fan', 'Salome', 'A Woman of No Importance', 'An Ideal Husband'* (Oxford, 1998), edited by Peter Raby, which includes the original scenario for 'Earnest'. There is a critical edition of *The Picture of Dorian Gray*, edited by Donald Lawler (New York, 1988). For *Teleny*, see Oscar Wilde and others, *Teleny, or the Reverse of the Medal* (London, 1986; reprinted 1999), introduced by John McRae.

For Wilde's correspondence, *The Complete Letters of Oscar Wilde*, edited by Merlin Holland and Rupert Hart-Davis (London, 2000) supersedes earlier editions. For occasional writings, see *The Artist as Critic: Critical Writings of Oscar Wilde*, edited by Richard Ellmann (Chicago, 1982) or *Selected Journalism*, edited by Anya Clayworth (Oxford, 2004). For juvenilia, see *Oscar Wilde's Oxford Notebooks: a Portrait of the Mind in the Making*, edited by Philip E. Smith II and Michael S. Helfand (New York / Oxford, 1989). This contains Wilde's 'Commonplace Book' and 'College Notebook'. A collection of anecdotes about and quotations purportedly by Wilde is *Oscar Wilde: Table Talk*, edited by Thomas Wright (London, 1988).

Date (for reasons of clarity, first performances of dramatic works are given in inverted commas; first publications, in London unless otherwise noted, in italics).

1878 'Ravenna' wins Newdigate Prize
1880 *Vera, or the Nihilists*
1881 *Poems*

1883 *Vera, or the Nihilists* first produced, New York

1885 'The Truth of Masks'

1887 'The Canterville Ghost'; 'The Sphinx without a Secret'; 'Lord Arthur Savile's Crime'; 'The Model Millionaire'

1888 *The Happy Prince and Other Tales*; 'The Young King'

1889 'The Decay of Lying'; 'Pen, Pencil and Poison'; 'The Birthday of the Infanta'; 'The Portrait of Mr W.H.'

1890 'The Picture of Dorian Gray' (in *Lippincott's Magazine*); 'The Critic as Artist'

1891 'The Duchess of Padua' first produced, New York, as 'Guido Ferranti'; 'The Soul of Man under Socialism'; *The Picture of Dorian Gray* (book form, with additional chapters and preface); *Intentions* (book collecting 'The Truth of Masks', 'The Critic as Artist', 'Pen, Pencil and Poison' and 'The Decay of Lying'); *Lord Arthur Savile's Crime and Other Stories* (book including 'The Canterville Ghost', 'The Sphinx without a Secret', 'Lord Arthur Savile's Crime' and 'The Model Millionaire'); *A House of Pomegranates* (including 'The Young King', 'The Birthday of the Infanta', 'The Fisherman and His Soul' and 'The Star Child')

1892 'Lady Windermere's Fan' produced, London; 'Salome' production banned

1893 *Teleny, or the Reverse of the Medal* (published anonymously); *Salome* (in French)
'A Woman of No Importance' produced, London; *Lady Windermere's Fan*

1894 *Salome* (in English translation by Lord Alfred Douglas, with illustrations by Aubrey Beardsley); *The Sphinx*; 'Poems in Prose'; *A Woman of No Importance*; 'A Few Maxims for the Instruction of the Over-Educated'; 'Phrases and Philosophies for the Use of the Young'

1895 'An Ideal Husband' produced, London; 'The Importance of Being Earnest' produced, London; *The Soul of Man under Socialism*

1896 'Salome' produced, Paris

1898 *The Ballad of Reading Gaol*, published as by 'C.3.3.'

1899 *The Importance of Being Earnest* (three-act version); *An Ideal Husband*

1905 *De Profundis* (expurgated edition published by Robbie Ross)

1908 First *Collected Edition* of Wilde's writings

1949 *De Profundis* (including suppressed passages; published by Vyvyan Holland)

1956 *The Importance of Being Earnest* (four-act version)

1962 *Collected Letters*, including first revised version of *De Profundis*

1986 *Teleny, or the Reverse of the Medal* (by 'Oscar Wilde and others')

Bibliography

The most detailed and impressive biography overall is still that published in 1987 by Richard Ellmann. However, it contains many inaccuracies, which have been comprehensively itemised by Horst Schroeder in his indispensable supplement to Ellmann. Some of Ellmann's comment in respect of Wilde's sexuality and relationships implies a lack of subtlety in respect of homosexuality. Some new discoveries and a welcome revision of this aspect of Ellmann are found in Neil McKenna's account. Merlin Holland's definitive 2003 volume of the trial against Queensberry supersedes previous editions. Hyde (1973) offers transcripts of the later prosecutions of Wilde of varying reliability.

The following have all been consulted:

Anne Clark Amor, *Mrs Oscar Wilde: a Woman of Some Importance* (London, 1983)

Neil Bartlett, *In Extremis* (London, 2001); *Who Was that Man?: a Present for Mr Oscar Wilde* (London, 1988)

Karl Beckson, *The Oscar Wilde Encyclopedia* (New York, 1998)

Karl Beckson (ed.), *Oscar Wilde: the Critical Heritage* (London, 1970)

Max Beerbohm, *Letters to Reggie Turner*, ed. Rupert Hart-Davis (London, 1964)

Patricia Flanagan Behrendt, *Oscar Wilde: Eros and Aesthetics* (London, 1991)

Barbara Belford, *Oscar Wilde: a Certain Genius* (London, 2000)

Martin Birnbaum, *Oscar Wilde: Fragments and Memories* (London, 1920)

Joseph Bristow, *Effeminate England: Homoerotic Writing after 1885* (Buckingham, 1995)

Joseph Bristow (ed.), *Wilde Writings: Contextual Conditions* (Toronto/Buffalo, New York/London, 2003)

Rhoda Broughton, *Second Thoughts* (London, 1880)

Julia Prewitt Brown, *Cosmopolitan Criticism: Oscar Wilde's Philosophy of Art* (Charlottesville, VA, 1997)

Stephen Calloway, *Aubrey Beardsley* (London, 1988)

Davis Coakley, *Oscar Wilde: the Importance of Being Irish* (Dublin, 1994)

H.G. Cocks, *Nameless Offences: Homosexual Desire in the Nineteenth Century* (London, 2003)

Ed Cohen, *Talk on the Wilde Side* (New York/London, 1993)

William A. Cohen, *Sex Scandal: the Private Parts of Victorian Fiction* (Durham/London, 1996)

Matt Cook, *London and the Culture of Homosexuality, 1885–1914* (Cambridge, 2003)

Rupert Croft-Cooke, *Bosie: the Story of Lord Alfred Douglas, His Friends and Enemies* (London, 1963); *The Unrecorded Life of Oscar Wilde* (London, 1972)

Lawrence Danson, *Wilde's Intentions: the Artist in his Criticism* (Oxford, 1997)

Jonathan Dollimore, *Sexual Dissidence: Augustine to Wilde, Freud to Foucault* (Oxford, 1991)

Denis Donoghue, *Walter Pater: Lover of Strange Souls* (London/New York, 1995)

Lord Alfred Douglas, *The Autobiography of Lord Alfred Douglas* (London, 1929); *Oscar Wilde and Myself* (London, 1914); *Oscar Wilde: a Summing Up* (London, 1940); *Without Apology* (London, 1938)

Terry Eagleton, *Saint Oscar* (London, 1990)

Richard Ellmann, *Oscar Wilde* (London, 1987)

Sos Eltis, *Revising Wilde: Society and Subversion in the Plays of Oscar Wilde* (Oxford, 1996)

Ronald Firbank, *The Artificial Princess* (London, 1934); *The Princess Zoubaroff* (London, 1920)

Trevor Fisher, *Oscar and Bosie: a Fatal Passion* (London, 2002)

Julia Constance Fletcher ('George Fleming'), *Mirage* (London, 1877)

Michael Foldy, *The Trials of Oscar Wilde: Deviance, Morality and Late-Victorian Society* (New Haven/London, 1997)

Nicholas Frankel, *Oscar Wilde's Decorated Books* (Ann Arbor, MI, 2000)

Jonathan Fryer, *André and Oscar: the Literary Friendship of André Gide and Oscar Wilde* (London, 1998); *Robbie Ross: Oscar Wilde's True Love* (London, 2000); *Wilde: Life and Times* (London, 2004)

Regenia Gagnier, *Idylls of the Marketplace: Oscar Wilde and the Victorian Public* (Stanford, CA, 1986)

Regenia Gagnier (ed.), *Critical Essays on Oscar Wilde* (Boston, 1991)

Lowell Gallagher, Frederick Roden and Patricia Juliana Smith (eds), *Catholic Figures, Queer Narratives* (Basingstoke/New York, 2007)

André Gide, *Oscar Wilde* (Paris, 1938)

Jonathan Goodman (ed.), *The Oscar Wilde File* (London, 1988)

Josephine Guy and Ian Small, *Oscar Wilde's Profession: Writing and the Culture Industry in the Late Nineteenth Century* (Oxford, 2000)

Ellis Hanson, *Decadence and Catholicism* (Cambridge, MA/London, 1998)

David Hare, *The Judas Kiss* (London, 1998)

Frank Harris, *Oscar Wilde, His Life and Confessions, including the hitherto unpublished 'Full and Final Confession' by Lord Alfred Douglas and 'My Memories of Oscar Wilde' by Bernard Shaw* (New York, 1930)

Robert Hichens, *The Green Carnation* (London, 1894)

Merlin Holland, *Irish Peacock and Scarlett Marquess: the Real Trial of Oscar Wilde* (London/New York, 2003); *The Wilde Album* (London, 1997)

Vyvyan Holland, *Son of Oscar Wilde* (London, 1954)

Hugh Montgomery Hyde, *Lord Alfred Douglas* (London, 1984); *Oscar Wilde: a Biography* (London, 1976); *The Trials of Oscar Wilde* (New York, 1973)

Joel Kaplan and Sheila Stowell, *Theatre and Fashion: Oscar Wilde to the Suffragettes* (Cambridge, 1988)

Morris Kaplan, *Sodom on the Thames: Sex, Love, and Scandal in Wilde Times* (Ithaca, NY/London, 2005)

Moises Kaufman, *Gross Indecency: the Three Trials of Oscar Wilde* (New York, 1998)

Melissa Knox, *Oscar Wilde: a Long and Lovely Suicide* (New Haven/London, 1994)

Norbert Kohl, *Oscar Wilde: the Works of a Conformist Rebel* (Cambridge, 1988)

Lillie Langtry, *The Days I Knew* (London, 1925)

Sally Ledger and Scott McCracken (eds), *Cultural Politics at the Fin de Siecle* (Cambridge, 1995)

Stuart Mason (pseudonym of Christopher Sclater Millard), *Bibliography of Oscar Wilde* (London, 1914; reprinted 1972)

[Stuart Mason], (published anon.), *Oscar Wilde: Three Times Tried* (London, [1912])

Jerusha Hull McCormack, *John Gray: Poet, Dandy and Priest* (Hanover, NH, 1991)

Jerusha Hull McCormack (ed.), *Wilde the Irishman* (New Haven/London, 1998)

Andrew McDonnell, *Oscar Wilde at Oxford: an Annotated Catalogue of Wilde Manuscripts and Related Items in the Bodleian Library* (Oxford, 1996)

Neil McKenna, *The Secret Life of Oscar Wilde* (London, 2003)

Joy Melville, *Mother of Oscar: the Life of Jane Francesca Wilde* (London, 1999)

E.H. Mikhail (ed.), *Oscar Wilde: Interviews and Recollections*, 2 vols. (London, 1979)

Douglas Murray, *Bosie: a Life of Lord Alfred Douglas* (London, 2000)

James Nelson, *Publisher to the Decadents: Leonard Smithers in the Careers of }Beardsley, Wilde, Dowson* (London, 2000)

H.W. Nevinson, *Changes and Chances* (London, 1923)

Max Nordau, *Degeneration* (orig. published in German, 1892; this edition 'translated from the second edition of the German Work', orig. New York, 1895; reprinted, Lincoln, NB/London, 1993), with an introduction by George L. Mosse

Jeff Nunokawa, *Tame Passions of Wilde: the Styles of Manageable Desire* (Princeton/Oxford, 2003)

Kevin O'Brien, *Oscar Wilde in Canada* (Toronto, 1982)

Hesketh Pearson, *The Life of Oscar Wilde* (London, 1946)

Richard Pine, *The Thief of Reason: Oscar Wilde and Modern Ireland* (Dublin, 1995)

Kerry Powell, *Oscar Wilde and the Theatre of the 1890s* (Cambridge, 1990)

Marquess of Queensberry and Percy Colson, *Oscar Wilde and the Black Douglas* (London, 1949)

Peter Raby, *Oscar Wilde* (Cambridge, 1988)

Peter Raby (ed.), *The Cambridge Companion to Oscar Wilde* (Cambridge, 1997)

Charles Ricketts, *Self-Portrait: taken from the Letters and Journals of Charles Ricketts, R.A.*, collected and compiled by T. Sturge Moore; ed. Cecil Lewis (London, 1939)

Charles Ricketts with Jean Paul Raymond, *Oscar Wilde: Recollections* (London, 1932)

Graham Robb, *Strangers: Homosexual Love in the Nineteenth Century* (London, 2003)

Brian Roberts, *The Mad, Bad Line: the Family of Lord Alfred Douglas* (London, 1981)

Frederick Roden, *Same-Sex Desire in Victorian Religious Culture* (New York, 2003)

Frederick Roden (ed.), *Palgrave Advances in Oscar Wilde Studies* (New York, 2004)

William Rothenstein, *Men and Memories* (New York, 1931)

Edgar Saltus, *Oscar Wilde: an Idler's Impression* (Chicago, 1917)

Neil Sammells, *Wilde Style: the Plays and Prose of Oscar Wilde* (London, 2000)

Christa Satzinger, *The French Influences on Oscar Wilde's 'The Picture of Dorian Gray' and 'Salomé'* (Lewiston, NY, 1994)

Joan Schenkar, *Truly Wilde: the Unsettling Story of Dolly Wilde, Oscar's Unusual Niece* (London, 2000)

Gary Schmidgall, *The Stranger Wilde: Interpreting Oscar* (New York/London, 1994)

Horst Schroeder, *Additions and Corrections to Richard Ellmann's Oscar Wilde* (second edition, Braunschweig, 2002)

Eve Kosofsky Sedgwick, *Epistemology of the Closet* (Berkeley, CA, 1990)

Brocard Sewell, *In the Dorian Mode: Life of John Gray, 1866–1934* (London, 1983)

Robert Harborough Sherard, *The Life of Oscar Wilde* (New York, 1906); *Oscar Wilde: the Story of an Unhappy Friendship* (London, 1902); *The Real Oscar Wilde* (London, [1915])

Alan Sheridan, *André Gide: a Life in the Present* (London, 1998)

Alan Sinfield, *The Wilde Century: Effeminacy, Oscar Wilde and the Queer Moment* (London, 1994)

John Sloan, *Oscar Wilde* (Oxford/New York) 2003

Ian Small, *Oscar Wilde Revalued: an Essay on New Materials and Methods of Research* (Greensboro, NC, 1993); *Oscar Wilde: Recent Research: a Supplement to 'Oscar Wilde Revalued'* (Greensboro, NC, 2000)

Philip E. Smith II and Michael S. Helfand (eds), *Oscar Wilde's Oxford Notebooks: a Portrait of the Mind in the Making* (New York/Oxford, 1989)

Julie Speedie, *Wonderful Sphinx: the Biography of Ada Leverson* (London, 1993)

John Stokes, *In the Nineties* (Hemel Hempstead, 1989); *Oscar Wilde: Myths, Miracles and Imitations* (Cambridge, 1996)

Tom Stoppard, *The Invention of Love* (London, 1997)

Matthew Sturgis, *Aubrey Beardsley: a Biography* (London, 1999)

Stanley Weintraub, *Reggie: a Portrait of Reginald Turner* (New York, 1965)

Chris White (ed.), *Nineteenth-Century Writings on Homosexuality: a Sourcebook* (New York/London, 1999)

Terence de Vere White, *The Parents of Oscar Wilde* (London, 1967)

Guy Willoughby, *Art and Christhood: the Aesthetics of Oscar Wilde* (London, 1993)

Frances Winwar, *Oscar Wilde and the Yellow Nineties* (London, 1940)

Katherine Worth, *Oscar Wilde* (London, 1983)

Theodore Wratislaw, *Oscar Wilde: a Memoir*, ed. Eighteen Nineties Society, with a foreword by Sir John Betjeman and an introduction and notes by Karl Beckson (London, 1979)

Horace Wyndham, *Speranza: a Biography of Lady Wilde* (New York, 1951)

W.B. Yeats, *Autobiography* (New York, 1965)

Biographical note

Richard Canning is Lecturer in English Literature at the University of Sheffield. He has published widely in the fields of gay literature and the literature of AIDS, including two books of conversations with gay novelists, *Gay Fiction Speaks* (New York, 2000) and the Lambda-award winning *Hear Us Out* (New York, 2003). He is editor of an anthology of gay male fiction, *Between Men* (New York, 2007) and a collection of AIDS fiction, *Vital Signs* (New York, 2007). His current projects include a critical life of Ronald Firbank and an edition of Louis Couperus' *Fate (Noodlot)*.

SELECTED TITLES FROM HESPERUS PRESS

Brief Lives

Classics and Modern Voices